PRAISE FOR
A LOVE LETTER LIFE

What your heart longs for most—is a love letter life. Hold these pages and fall the way you've always wanted. Jeremy and Audrey have vulnerably written their own tender love story that will powerfully awaken you to write your own rare kind of love story—the kind of love letter life that just keeps falling more deeply into a sacred intimacy.

Ann Voskamp, *New York Times* bestselling author
of *One Thousand Gifts* and *The Broken Way*

We're so grateful for Jeremy and Audrey's story that they so graciously and honestly lay out in *A Love Letter Life*. It's one of those rare books that makes you feel like you're having dinner or coffee with them, while simultaneously gaining a wealth of knowledge and wisdom and things to think about! We'll be passing out copies to friends, for sure.

Jefferson and Alyssa Bethke,
New York Times bestselling authors of
Jesus > Religion and *Love That Lasts*

Jeremy and Audrey's beautiful love story is one founded on the true source of hope and life, Jesus Christ. Their timeless tale is one of adventure, creativity, and faith, available for not just them but all of us when we allow God to be the center and foundation of our relationships. Read and be inspired to know that with intentionality, you too can live a love letter life.

John and Lisa Bevere, bestselling authors

A Love Letter Life will inspire you, challenge you, and guide you to an intentional marriage. What a gift this book is to hearts that are longing for what lasts!

Lara Casey, author of *Make It*
Happen and *Cultivate*

It's no surprise that most of the Bible comes to us as history and biography. In reading other people's stories, we discover our own. More than that, we navigate our own path by the landmarks of those who have gone before us. Jeremy and Audrey Roloff have done a superb job of walking the road of dating to marriage, not just as lovers of each other, but as followers of Jesus. They take their relationship seriously; they take Jesus even more seriously. There is much to learn in these pages.

John Mark Comer, pastor of teaching and vision
at Bridgetown Church in Portland, Oregon, and
author of "The Ruthless Elimination of Hurry"

While reading *A Love Letter Life*, I felt as if I was reading a story that should be on the big screens! Audrey and Jeremy know that love is about action, and not passive feelings. I admire them for the way they live their lives, and I'm thankful they are in this world to showcase what true love is about.

Chelsea Crockett, Encounter Now podcast with
Nick and Chels, author of *Your Own Beautiful*

A Love Letter Life is inspiring! Reading Jeremy and Audrey's story refueled our desire as a couple to continually pursue our marriage with intentional ways of creatively expressing our love for each other. We appreciated their candid way of sharing such intimate moments from their relationship, using their experience to encourage others who are on the journey of dating, engaged or already married! This is a modern-day classic romantic love story that will be the kindling in couples' hearts that sparks deep love for years to come.

Aaron and Jennifer Smith, authors
of *Marriage After God*

The Roloffs share their inspiring love story packed with humor, struggles, romance, and wisdom. Be sure to read with a highlighter or pen nearby! *A Love Letter Life* is full of wisdom and truth bombs about how to pursue a love that lasts.

Jason Kennedy, *E! News* host

Jeremy and Audrey Roloff are beautiful storytellers, and their genuine respect and love for each other leaps off the pages of *A Love Letter Life*. Wherever you're at in your love story, this book will inspire and equip you to pursue a love story you'd want to read about someday.

Scott Harrison, *New York Times*
bestselling author of *Thirst*

Inviting, authentic, and compassionate, the Roloffs speak to the longing heart. As they take us on a journey through their love story, we are challenged to live a story worth writing about. This book provides not only the inspiration but also the tools and ideas to make it a reality.

Jordan Lee Dooley, author,
founder of the SoulScripts movement,
and host of the SHE podcast

A LOVE
LETTER
Life

A LOVE LETTER *Life*

PURSUE CREATIVELY. DATE INTENTIONALLY.
LOVE FAITHFULLY.

JEREMY AND AUDREY ROLOFF

To Ember Jean

May you be a light in this world.

We love you,
Mom and Dad

CONTENTS

OUR FIRST
Letter

AUDREY

It was a storybook summer. We spent our days walking train tracks, riding in truck beds, sneaking through train tunnels, jumping off bridges, picking berries, playing fugitive, climbing hay bales, exploring old barns, playing harmonicas, watching drive-in movies, and losing track of time. We capped off nearly every evening by the campfire pit, permanently saturating our clothes with the smell of smoked Pacific Northwest pine and sacrificing sleep to be together—even when togetherness meant simply sitting in silence and waiting for the sound of the train to echo through the rolling hills of Helvetia, Oregon. As the country song goes, this was the "summer I turned a corner in my soul."[1] It was a summer unhindered by time and full of adventure. It was the summer I finally let myself fall for the farm boy who had patiently pursued me for two years. It was a summer of "winning moments" that consistently affirmed we were falling in love.

As September drew near, our summer of timeless perfection was coming to a close, and we both had different finish lines. I was heading back to college at Oregon State in Corvallis for preseason cross-country training, and Jeremy was transferring from Portland Community College to Brooks Institute of film and photography in Santa Barbara, California. All summer, we had chosen to ignore the fact that our relationship would eventually be complicated by 900 miles of separation. It made the fifteen-minute commute from my parents' house in the suburbs to Jeremy's family farm in the country seem like nothing. We both anticipated a defining good-bye, but neither of us was sure if it would mark the end of a summer love or the beginning of a lifelong love story.

In the weeks leading up to Jeremy's departure, we felt increasing pressure to have the DTR—the *define the relationship* talk. We both agreed we needed to talk about expectations for our relationship before we went back to school. Would we be just friends? Would we begin a long-distance dating relationship? Or would we just raise our glasses to an epic summer and move on?

After heading home from another evening by the campfire, I got a text from Jeremy. Auj, we need to talk about what we are going to do.

I knew what he meant. Yes, we do.

Tomorrow, I'll pick you up around five, and we'll go to the trestle to talk. We won't leave without discussing the future of our relationship.

With butterflies in my stomach I typed, Sounds like a plan.

That night, I nervously scribbled my unfiltered thoughts in my journal. All summer, I had been praying for discernment in anticipation of the day we would inevitably have the DTR. For me, there was a lot more riding on our conversation than whether or not Jeremy and I would officially start dating. Two years previously, I had made a commitment to myself that I wouldn't enter a serious dating relationship with someone I couldn't see myself marrying. That made saying yes to dating feel like saying yes to Jeremy for the rest of my life.

Looking back, despite all my efforts to be intentional, I realize that in some ways I had put too much pressure on dating. After all, how are you going to figure out if someone is worth marrying if you avoid or turn down every guy who looks your way? Maybe I needed to be more willing to experience a few awkward no's before I found my yes.

When I woke up the next morning, I analyzed every possible outcome of our conversation. Would he ask me to be his girlfriend despite the long distance? Or would we shy away from that level of commitment and agree to just "see what happens"? We were both aware of all that was riding on our conversation, which made the hours leading up to our DTR feel like days. Unlike our summer of timeless days, this day was completely pressured by hard-stop time— our five o'clock meeting and our impending back-to-school dates.

I heard the rumble of Blue Moon accelerating into my neighborhood long before it reached my street. Blue Moon was Jeremy's rusty, dented, pale blue Volkswagen van. Every time I heard Blue Moon—or any of Jeremy's old cars—pull up to my house, my heart beat faster and my hands grew shaky.

Even though I could hear him coming from a mile away, I waited upstairs for him to park and come to my door. Unlike most guys I had dated, Jeremy never sat in his car and texted, I'm here. He always came to the door and knocked. When I opened the door this time, I could have sworn he'd gotten cuter overnight, which spiked my nerves and my heart rate even more. We greeted each other with blushed faces and flirtatious smiles. Jeremy walked me over to the van and opened the door for me. As he did, he said, "Hey, we should try to throw our shoes before we talk. I brought them!"

Jeremy and I had decided we wanted to timestamp our summer in a concrete way. True to unconventional form, we had this idea to tie together two of our old shoes—one of his and one of mine—and toss them over a wire under our beloved train trestle, one of the longest wooden train bridges in North America. The train trestle had become "our spot" that summer, and we wanted to leave our mark. Although we didn't say it out loud, I think we both hoped that the shoes would become a forever reminder of the summer we began a lifelong love story. "Oh yeah!" I blurted. "I'm glad you remembered!" This quirky task calmed my nerves. Now we had something else to do besides have "the talk."

Our nerves made for a pretty quiet twelve-minute drive to the bridge. Once we arrived, Jeremy parked Blue Moon on the gravel road just up the way from the trestle. He opened the side door of the van, and we sat on the floorboard prepping for our shoe mission. We firmly tied our shoelaces together, and on the bottom of one of Jer's shoes we wrote, "Jer and Auj summer 2011." Then we walked the quarter mile to the opening in the railroad beams where the bridge arches over the road. This is where we had scouted the perfect spot to throw our shoes in hopes that they wouldn't be easily discovered and would be nearly impossible to take down.

A thin wire ran underneath the railroad tracks about sixty feet up. As we stood beneath it, I felt only a grim hope that we would accomplish this mission successfully. In contrast, Jeremy looked up at the wire with confident assurance. He immediately kicked off his Birkenstocks and began climbing up the wooden beams, staining his feet with creosote as he ascended. Once he reached a beam with a good tossing angle, he launched the shoes at the wire. One of the shoes struck a beam, sending them ricocheting back down onto the hot summer blacktop.

I quickly retrieved them and tried to fling them back up to Jeremy, but my aim proved horrible. Jeremy had to climb down and then go back up again. This time before throwing our shoes, he closed his eyes and playfully prayed, "Lord, help me make this!" On his second attempt, the laces caught the wire perfectly, and the shoes wrapped around it multiple times. *He did it!* I was stunned. I've always been wary of signs, but the shoes sure did feel like one. Jer climbed down, and we stared up at our shoes with pride, both of us secretly hoping this would be a permanent symbol of a beginning rather than an end.

We walked back through the unharvested grass fields that surrounded the trestle beams and up a sloping hill until we reached the top of the tracks. We sat on the sun-warmed rails, and Jeremy suggested we start our conversation with prayer. We bowed our heads. I don't remember everything he said, but I do remember he prayed for the Lord's will in our relationship.

As we said amen and lifted our heads, I felt simultaneously hot and cold—a rush of heat filled my face, and I was frozen with nervousness. I'm usually a pretty decisive person. I pride myself on being a fast outfit picker, and I'm always the first to order at a restaurant, but when it came to dating, I experienced a change in cabin pressure. I knew that dating Jeremy meant three years in a long-distance relationship, and I felt apprehensive about the burden that long distance might become. Doubts swirled in my mind. I was afraid that the distance might ruin our love story. Would we have a better chance at forever if we just stayed friends until we could be in the same city again? I liked Jeremy. He was husband material, and I was beginning to envision a future with him, but what if it was just bad timing? I had spent the morning journaling and praying about how to express my concerns to him, but in the moment, I couldn't recall any of them. To my relief, Jeremy initiated the conversation.

He started out by recapping our glorious summer. We both beamed with joy as we relived all the memories we had made. Then there was a pause. With a more serious tone, Jeremy looked me in the eyes and said, "I know we both said we would never do long distance, but I think I'll always wonder what could have been if we don't at least try. I don't want to look back on this summer as just a blissful memory with that girl I once knew. Audrey, when I go off to school in Santa Barbara, I want to be able to call you mine. Will you be my girlfriend?"

"Yes!" I said with my whole heart. While he was talking, an overwhelming sense of peace had come over me. All the worries and uncertainties I'd had about being in a long-distance relationship suddenly vanished. We sat in silence for a moment, realizing that this marked the culmination of a two-year patient pursuit. Although we didn't know it at the time, it also marked the beginning of an ongoing pursuit for the rest of our lives.

Bursting with adrenaline, we held hands as we trekked back down the sloping hill into the now starlit fields. When we reached the road beneath the trestle, Jeremy stopped and suggested we take in the night sky for a moment. We lay down on the pavement and gazed up. There was a full moon that night, but it was a massive shooting star racing across the sky that forever sealed the moment in our memories.

Finally we were officially dating, but we only had ten days before

Jeremy had to leave for school. We savored every minute together during those ten days and ended each night by the campfire pit. We held hands, shared our first kiss, and gave voice to the thoughts we'd had about each other but had concealed for so long. As we talked by the campfire on Jer's last night, we committed to writing letters to each other. Yes, *letters*. Real pen and ink on paper, folded into stamped envelopes. We wanted *more* than text messages and nightly phone calls. We had a deep desire to add excitement and creativity to our communication and also to chronicle the growth of our love. Letters seemed perfect.

On August 25, 2011, Jeremy left for his new home in Santa Barbara. I drove to his house to watch Blue Moon kick up dust as it rumbled down the long gravel driveway at Roloff Farms, packed to the brim with his belongings. Before we said one of our first drawn-out good-byes, Jeremy handed me my first letter. It was wax-sealed in an old brown envelope. I felt like a starlet on the set of a 1950s romance movie. He asked me to wait to read it until after he had left and then to mail my response to his new apartment in Santa Barbara. He wanted something to look forward to. Holding his first letter made me feel like I was holding the immunity idol in *Survivor*. I wasn't naive to the fact that we would endure many Tribal Councils in our years of long distance, but something about holding that first letter gave me confidence that our torches would keep burning.

In our final moments before good-bye, we both felt a whole gamut of conflicting emotions. Unsure, yet confident. Nervous, yet at peace. Heartbroken, yet excited. One thing we wholeheartedly agreed on was that love wouldn't just happen to us. We had to pursue it. We were committed to writing our own God-inspired love story. Jeremy's first letter was the start of our love letter life.

Audrey,

Well, this is the beginning. Such an amazing feeling. I just want to say I am really excited. I am looking forward to our next chapter as God is on our side. I will be praying for you and for us.

I really want you to speak your mind with me. I want to know what you're thinking. It makes me feel better because I didn't know for so long.

As always there is so much I want to say to you, but I just get lost in my thoughts. It's okay though. We have plenty of writing to do. And Skype!

I feel the need to emphasize the concept of being open with each other through this process. We went two years with keeping things bottled up, which I believe worked out for the better, but it might have become a habit. However, we're dating now, so the rules have changed. If something bugs you, let me know.

We had so much fun this summer, Auj. I really enjoyed getting to know you more. One of these days, we will get our notes and thoughts together and write a screenplay, or a book!

Well, I'm gonna keep this one short because I don't have time (you're on your way over). If you ever cannot read or understand what I'm saying, text me, or we will Skype-date it.

You're beautiful.

THE
BEGINNING

JEREMY

Two years earlier, I almost missed my chance to meet Audrey. It was during winter break of my freshman year of college when I received a text from an old friend named Mitch: Jer, I have someone you need to meet. A girl. You free Saturday?

I was still recovering from a failed three-year relationship, and this wasn't the first time a friend had tried to set me up. I promptly shut him down. Hey, man, good to hear from you. No, I'm busy. Sorry!

This happened during the peak of *Little People, Big World*, a reality television show about my family that had been airing for five years at the time. I had gotten used to people asking me to meet friends and friends of friends. I always felt uncertain about the motives behind the meetings, so I rarely obliged. However, Mitch was a good friend, an old friend who had my trust, and he insisted.

Reluctantly, I agreed to a blind date with some girl named Audrey. What made me say yes? I still don't know. I spent the rest of the week looking for reasons to bail, even up to the last minute. Before I could cancel, Mitch texted me the address of Audrey's parents' house. It was just a couple hours before we were supposed to meet up, so I was too far in to back out now.

That evening, I tried on five different outfits before I climbed into OhSo, my little orange 1971 BMW 2002, and headed down the misty driveway. Although I was reluctant to go, there was something thrilling about going on a date with someone I knew nothing about, and I wanted to make a good impression. I arrived ten minutes early and parked across the street from Audrey's parents' house. The front lawn was perfectly manicured. A brick archway stretched thirty feet high and framed the front door, which was covered with perfectly arranged Christmas decorations. A fluffy white cat was perched in an upstairs window and looked down at me as though he knew what I was in for. Everything seemed too tidy. *Goodness, she's probably a straight-A student type*, I thought. *Awkward. Boring. High-maintenance.* Now I felt even more apprehensive.

I had never gone on a blind date before, and to be honest, it just felt embarrassing. I wasn't desperate. I was doing this for a friend because I trusted him and he had insisted. I was convinced there was no way sparks would fly and zero chance I'd hit it off with some random girl from the burbs.

I walked up to the front door, knocked, and waited. No answer, no sounds of stirring, nothing. I raised my hand to give it another knock when—*shebang!*—the door flew open while my hand was still in midair. Before me stood a girl with frizzy red hair wearing running buns and a sports bra. Her petite frame was dripping with sweat and speckled with mud. *What in the world kind of girl opens the door dressed like this when meeting a complete stranger?* She was slender and pretty and had a big smile on her face. I thought she was probably expecting me to be Kelcey, Mitch's girlfriend and one of Audrey's best friends, who was going to be joining us.

"Hi," I said, "are you Audrey?" Some part of me hoped this mess-of-a-girl was Audrey's sister or something.

"Yeah, hi!" she said. "You're Jeremy. Nice to meet you. Sorry, I'm running a little behind. Kelcey and Mitch aren't here yet, but come on in." The words flew out of her mouth almost as fast as the run she'd apparently just finished.

"No worries, I know I'm a bit early."

The words were barely out of my mouth before she turned around and bolted up the stairs, calling back something like, "I'll be ready in a few. Just wait in the kitchen and . . ."

Her voice trailed off as she rounded the corner. Still standing in the doorway, I let myself in the house, took off my shoes, and placed them neatly next to the others under the entryway bench. I found my way to the kitchen and sat down. *Well, this is awkward.* Looking around the house, I concluded that the family seemed normal enough. The house was clean and organized; sports trophies lined the shelves; Scripture cards were posted on the fridge; and a tray of homemade desserts filled the counter. *Okay, maybe this won't be too bad.*

A few minutes later, to my relief, there was a knock at the door. Before I could get up, I heard the door open and shut and someone kick off their shoes. From around the corner walked Kelcey. I knew of Kelcey, but we hadn't met. Mitch and Kelcey had been dating for a while, and both had gone to high school with Audrey. Kelcey was in Audrey's tight group of best friends, whom I would later come to know as "the God Squad."

Mitch showed up a few minutes later and joined us at the kitchen table. While we chatted about the plan for the evening, I got the feeling Mitch and Kelcey both had higher expectations than I did. The plan was to eat dinner at the local Macaroni Grill—where we were sure to engage in some thrilling conversation—before heading to the opening service of Solid Rock. Solid Rock was the church they all attended, and a new campus was launching that night in downtown Portland. I had been there occasionally, but I was in a season of spiritual complacency and wasn't regularly reading my Bible or committed to a church.

Audrey eventually walked down the stairs, and I looked over from across the room as she approached the kitchen table. Her beautiful red hair was pulled to the side and cascaded down the front of her floral ruffled blouse. She wore black leggings that formed to her athletic legs, and black lace-up boots. Her lips shimmered with a generous gloss of red lipstick. *Okay, fine, she's hot.*

We all piled into Audrey's red Mazda and headed off to dinner. When the server came to take our drink order, Audrey casually looked up from her menu and said, "I'll take a glass of milk."

Milk? Who is this girl? Who orders milk at a restaurant . . . and on a blind date!

Over dinner, we talked about a wide range of topics, and I found myself both perplexed and intrigued by Audrey. Her thoughts, interests, and mannerisms were peculiar, and I couldn't get a read on her. She was unlike any girl I had ever met. Our curiosity was mutual. She would later say she felt she had met the boy version of herself—that I was quirky like her and we were interested in many of the same things. Prompted by Mitch, we discovered that we even shared the same favorite movie—*Stand by Me*. There was no neat box I could fit this girl into. And there was zero mention of *Little People, Big World*. The show was usually one of the first things—and sometimes the only thing—that people I'd just met wanted to talk about. That alone threw me off guard and piqued my interest.

After dinner, we headed to church, where I met the rest of the God Squad. When I asked about the name, they explained that some boy in middle school had called them the God Squad as a way to poke fun, but the name had stuck.

The service was routine—pray, sing, sermon, pray again—but there was a lot of energy in the room. Everyone was excited to celebrate the beginning of this new campus. I, however, was pre-occupied with this unusual girl and also a little self-conscious, knowing that her best friends and Mitch and Kelcey were constantly looking in our direction to see if anything was happening between Audrey and me.

After church, we drove back to Audrey's place and said our good-byes. It wasn't a sparks-flying kind of night, and yet something about it had felt so right.

I was curious about this girl. She clearly marched to the beat of her own drum. I liked that. Her confidence and strong sense of herself were refreshing. Something about our meeting felt "meant to be." Even though I couldn't get a good read on her, there were uncanny moments when I felt a deep sense of connection and a longing for more.

Who is this girl?

I decided to press on and find out. That blind date marked the beginning of my patient pursuit of Audrey Mirabella Botti.

1

A PATIENT
Pursuit

AUDREY

I couldn't stop thinking about the skinny jean–wearing, Taylor Swift–loving, vintage car–driving farm boy. A few months had passed since our blind date at Macaroni Grill, and although I wasn't ready to be in a serious relationship, I was definitely curious about this boy. Over the next few months, whenever I was home from school for the weekend, Jeremy and I would rendezvous at church. Sometimes he met up with my friends and me ahead of time so we could drive together. Other times, he hung out with us after church for some late-night grub. While I was at school, Jeremy would send an occasional text with a movie, podcast, or song suggestion, but we hadn't gone on a second date or spent any time alone together. When I came home for summer break and it was warm enough to hang outside in the evenings, he invited me over to the farm for the first time.

I approached the iconic Roloff Farms sign on Helvetia Road, turned down the gravel driveway, and proceeded to the dimly lit security gate. I glanced down at my phone to review Jeremy's text message instructions outlining which buttons to press on the keypad. After I pressed a few buttons, Jeremy's voice crackled back through the intercom.

"Auj?"

"It's me!"

"Access granted," announced a robotic voice as the gate opened, although it felt as if in that same moment I also granted access to my heart in some small way.

I followed the driveway through a tunnel of trees that led up to an enormous farmhouse. As I pulled up, a large group of guys and girls all hopped onto a giant passenger ATV thing and then sped off. I took a few deep breaths in the comfort zone of my car before emerging. Jeremy was standing outside and motioned for me to join him on a smaller ATV.

"Hop on the mule," he said. "Everyone is headed out to the campfire pit."

Mule? I knew he must be referring to the ATV, but I felt like an idiot for not being more fluent in farm lingo. I joined him on the mule, and we buzzed past barns, farm equipment, animals, and other structures I couldn't quite make out in the dark. We reached the campfire pit where Zach, Jeremy's twin brother, was debriefing the rest of the gang on the rules. Unless you're a *Little People, Big World* fan, you'd never know that Zach is Jeremy's twin brother. They look and act nothing alike.

We were about to play a game of Fugitive, but this was different from the suburban style Fugitive I was used to playing with my friends. For us public school kids, Fugitive was essentially a giant game of tag, but the people who are "it" are "cops" and drive around in cars. We usually designated four cop cars, with multiple people in each car. Everyone else was a "fugitive." For the fugitives, the goal was to run from the starting location (usually a school parking lot), to the destination (usually another school parking lot), without getting tagged by the cops. Sometimes that required running through surrounding neighborhoods or parks to stay out of sight. To officially catch the fugitives, cops had to pull over, get out of the car, and tag them. Fugitives who got caught became cops and had to help catch other fugitives. The first person to make it to the destination without getting caught won the game.

I took pride in my fugitive skills. Even when I was spotted, I could always outrun the cops. But the rules for Farm Fugitive turned out to be much different. When you grow up on thirty-four acres, you don't need to run through people's backyards and apartment complexes in order to play the game. Instead of cop cars, Zach drove around on a mule while the rest of us fugitives ran from one end of the farm to the other, and back again. Instead of having to actually get out and tag us, Zach just had to call out our names. That meant stealth was even more important than speed.

As Zach pointed out the boundary lines, I felt my confidence begin to plummet. Apparently, we were all supposed to run from the campfire pit to the pumpkin barn, which was a safe zone, and then back to the campfire pit. Except I had no idea where the pumpkin barn was.

Before I could ask any questions, Zach was counting down, and everyone took off running. I followed Jeremy into the dark forest and immediately felt disoriented. Within a minute or so, we could hear the mule closing in on us. Jeremy and his friend Mueller quickly vaulted over a fence that took me much longer to scale. By the time my feet hit the ground, the boys were long gone, and I was left to navigate Roloff Farms on my own.

This was no ordinary farm. I felt like I was running through a farm version of Disneyland. I ran through the forest past a swamp fort; over a hill inhabited by sheep, goats, and cows accompanied by a replica of Noah's ark; through a miniature cowboy town; past a pirate ship, a *Swiss Family Robinson* tree house, a castle, and a sports arena; and through fields of hay, berries, and flowers. Even in the dark, I was enamored with it all.

For a while, I wondered if I would find the pumpkin barn before dawn, but I was eventually able to make out some pumpkin paraphernalia in the dark, a few signs for tours, and a maze of wooden fences that I guessed to be some kind of line management system for the pumpkin business. When I finally reached the safe zone—the barn—I was congratulated by Jeremy and Mueller.

"Auj, you made it! We're gonna make a run for it up the High Road; come with us!"

As soon as Zach's mule crested over "Roloff Mountain" and dropped down behind "Barn Three," we sprinted through the pumpkin arena and up a massive hill toward what I assumed to be the edge of the property. Even though I was breathing hard, I couldn't help but smile. The enchantment of this place and the wonder of this farm boy had already captured a piece of my heart.

We made it to the campfire pit unspotted and unscathed. We won! A few moments later, we were reunited with the rest of the fugitives, all of whom had been spotted and become cops. We laughed, shared our stories of escape or capture, and hung out by the fire. After everyone else eventually went home, I stayed. Lingering as the minutes turned to hours.

Jeremy and I talked and stared into the embers, occasionally lifting our gazes to make eye contact through the flames. I questioned him about all the unorthodox structures I'd encountered as a fugitive, and he downloaded on me the genesis of the farm and the story behind all of its artifacts.

"Was any of this here when your parents bought the property?" I asked. "What made your parents want to build this crazy playground?"

The question put a twinkle in Jer's eye. He stood up to tell the story. "When my dad was a kid, he had several surgeries on his legs. While he was recovering in the hospital, he dreamed of having adventures with cowboys, Indians, knights, and pirates. When he and my mom bought the farm, he finally got the chance to bring all of those childhood dreams to life. Zach, Molly, Jacob, and I grew up playing cowboys and Indians in a mini cowboy town, playing knights in the castle, walking the plank on the pirate ship, and sleeping in our *Swiss Family Robinson* tree house." He smiled as he spoke. I could see how much he cherished this place.

"Wow, that's insane!" I said, eager to hear the rest of the story.

Jeremy described his childhood as every kid's dream. His parents, who are dwarfs, bought the farm when Jeremy and his twin brother Zach were still in the womb. It was just a rolling piece of land in the Oregon countryside, but Jer's dad had a vision for what it would one day become.

Throughout Jer's childhood, his parents not only built the playground and tourist attraction that is now Roloff Farms, but they also renovated the old farmhouse and started the family pumpkin business. The fact that they did all of this as little people managing a giant farm while simultaneously raising four children was what eventually caught the attention of a few television networks.

I assumed the TV show helped to build everything that was on the farm, but it was just the opposite. It was everything on the farm that helped catch the attention of the television networks.

"It really was, and still is, a magical place," Jeremy said with gratitude. "Honestly, the farm has been like a third parent to me. It's taught me so much and made me who I am today."

I was eager to know more—about the farm and about the boy who had been so impacted by it. This was the first of many nights we would spend together by the campfire pit that summer. Even so, I wasn't looking for a serious relationship. My priorities were elsewhere, and falling in love felt far-fetched to me. I never got too caught up in longing for romance or seeking attention from guys. I was content on my own and took pride—perhaps too much of it—in my independence.

I liked that my relationship status was not an indicator of my happiness or well-being. But the more time I spent with Jeremy, the more I started to wonder if this could ever be more than friendship. I remember thinking, *If this ever does develop into something, what an amazing story we will be able to tell!*

JEREMY

I knew from the start that Audrey was a special girl, someone I wanted to pursue and hopefully build a love story with. She seemed to have the fruit of the Spirit in her life that the apostle Paul describes in Galatians 5: love, joy, peace, patience, kindness, goodness, faithfulness, gentleness, and self-control. But I also knew that pursuing her meant I needed to get my act together. If I hoped to have even a shot at making this girl mine, I needed to become the kind of man who was deserving of her. At the time, I was in a season of laziness, losing sight of who I was becoming and what I was doing. Meeting Audrey was a firm reality check. So I got to work—on myself.

I dusted off my Bible and immersed myself in truths about the kind of person I wanted to become—a man of discipline, purity, and direction who pursued a deeper relationship with Jesus. Until Audrey, I had never met someone who held up a mirror to my life just by being herself. The light in her life showed me not only who I was, but also who I wanted to be. She inspired me to become a better person. The pursuit was on.

It was clear skies and warm weather. Spring had sprung, and our crew of friends decided it would be a good night to head to "the clearing" for a bonfire. The clearing, as we dubbed it, was a half-logged sloping hill, the remnant of a logging operation that had been abandoned for quite some time. It was just a few miles north of the farm. The east side of the hill that faces North Portland is logged, leaving a beautiful lookout over the Willamette River where it snakes around Sauvie Island.

Excited to make another memory, I called Audrey and asked if she wanted to come with me that evening. "There's something I want to show you. Meet up with us at the farm tonight?" Her only question was, "What time?" I liked her go-with-the-flow personality and her willingness to embrace the element of surprise.

When she arrived at the farm, the rest of us were already loaded into the farm's pickup truck. Zach was behind the wheel; Roth and Scott were in the front seat of the cab; Dan and Jake were in the back seat; and Mueller and I were in the truck bed. Country Rule #37 says, "Never pass up an opportunity to ride in a truck bed," and we tried our best to abide by the Country Rules.

Audrey jumped in the back of the cab, and I hollered up to Zach, "Good to go!"

The truck was packed with all the ingredients for a good time— firewood, blankets, and a full cooler. We also brought along a guitar in hopes that Roth, our designated musician, would indulge us with some songs. Once we arrived at the clearing, we started walking up the trail to the point where it would eventually fork. The typical hiker always chose to go straight at the fork, but we peeled off to the right—on the trail that led to a hidden spot we had discovered the previous summer. With the fire lit, blankets laid out, and the sun setting, we talked into the night. Mueller talked about his latest girlfriend; Roth told stories about his customers at the local Linens-'n-Things; Zach went on some soccer rant; and we all razzed him about his trunkful of Mountain Dew cans. The night was lighthearted, and we felt young.

At one point, I walked a hundred feet or so down the hill to take a tinkle (Audrey *still* laughs at me when I use this word). As I was walking back, I met Audrey on the trail. My heart skipped a beat, and I suddenly got all nervous. Finding myself alone with her sent a jolt of electricity through me.

"Hey, how you doing?" I asked. It was the best I could come up with on short notice.

"I'm good," she said, "but I have to pee too!"

I started to explain that there were no Porta Potties, but she quickly cut me off. Evidently, there was no time to waste.

"I don't need one," she said. "Can I go where you went?"

Oddly enough, this impressed me. A girl who is down to pee in the woods—radical!

"Yes, of course!" I said, pointing to the general area. "I'll wait for you around the corner."

When she emerged from the forest, we moseyed back up the hill. The Milky Way lit our path, and we paused to admire its brilliance. I glanced over at her and whispered, "This is what I wanted to show you." We stood together in silence. There was peace in the cool night air.

I can't remember how long we admired the sky, but we eventually made our way back up to the firepit, where we were greeted by a hoot and holler from Mueller. Apparently, our absence had been noted. Laughing off our embarrassment, we joined the group in putting out the fire and loading up the truck.

On the ride back, seemingly by accident—although such things rarely are—it was just Audrey and me who ended up sitting in the truck bed. We were quiet most of the way, but it was the farthest thing from awkward. In fact, it was a silent joy. Nothing needed to be said. Never had silence felt so comfortable. We sat next to each other and leaned against the cab of the truck. The trees zipped past as the road behind us disappeared around every turn.

I wanted to kiss her, but we hadn't even confessed our feelings for each other. If I did, I would be admitting my feelings for her, and it felt too soon—or was it? I knew I was falling in love, but I also knew the principle that it's wise to be patient when pursuing someone you don't want to lose. I didn't want a kiss to determine the status of our relationship or confuse my feelings for her. I didn't need a kiss—I knew that. And if I was going to kiss her, I wanted to do it on the foundation of a friendship that could support it. I knew we weren't there yet, so I refrained. Barely.

Our relationship grew quite a bit that night. We were two friends getting to know one another without the pressure of the "boyfriend/girlfriend" label. We were becoming friends while also beginning to fall madly in love—but patiently.

As spring became summer, we spent more and more time together. What some would call "friend-zoned," I called pursuit. I got to know Audrey, and she got to know me. We developed increasing levels of trust, joy, respect, and admiration for one another. I got to see how she treated her parents, what she was interested in, what her hopes and dreams were, and the strength of her faith. There was a growing excitement of discovery between us. I was in hot pursuit—crafting gifts for her, taking her places, and spending time with her.

Now, to be honest, not everything I experienced with Audrey at this point was a positive. I discovered that she had quite a few walls around her heart. I started to notice her walls more and more as our friendship grew. She seemed to be into me, but she wouldn't—or maybe couldn't—hint at something more than just friendship.

I took the fact that she kept hanging out with me to be a good sign, but Audrey was a hard nut to crack. Her strong will kept her distant and difficult to read. Part of my patient pursuit included attempting to carefully break through her walls. As we continued to spend time together, I pursued her creatively and patiently. I think a girl like Audrey was a hard catch because she wasn't interested in men, but a man. I wanted to be that man, the one who fought for her heart.

At times it was very difficult, but I continued to pursue her because, deep down, I believed that what we were experiencing was mutual. There was an intensity between us, an *inloveness*, that invited both vulnerability and caution. We were careful with one another because we didn't want to mess it up. This friendship we were nurturing allowed us to build the foundation for a love story without getting lost in a cloud of emotions from physical intimacy.

I believed that if I kept pursuing her, Audrey was a treasure worth waiting for.

A word to the single guys out there. If you're pursuing a woman who is hard to catch, don't give up! It means she has standards, and she isn't about to fall for just any guy with a smartphone who sends her heart emojis. If you're serious about wanting a lifelong relationship with this woman, your patient pursuit is part of what qualifies you as husband material.

Pursuit takes work, and so does marriage. If you learn to pursue before you say "I do," it's a skill that will continue to serve you well beyond the *I do*. When the real thing hits you, pursuit itself becomes a pleasure. I wanted nothing more than to find a way to Audrey's heart. I was eager to press in, and doing so made me feel alive. I wanted more, and if you're reading this book, I'm guessing you do too. So take a risk and press in! Just don't get weird. You don't want to end up on the creeper list. Pursuit is politely persistent.

My patient pursuit was the scariest thing I had ever done, but it was also the most exhilarating. There were times I was tempted to cower in the corner with fear of rejection, but if I did, I'd lose her. Audrey was the type of girl I wanted to take a few arrows of rejection for to have a chance at love with. Rejection is temporary; the glory of true love is eternal! As the wise King Solomon said, "He who finds a wife finds a good thing" (Proverbs 18:22 ESV). However, he never said it would be easy! On rare occasions, this finding may fall into your lap with a note from God attached that reads, "You're welcome." Kind of like how I met Audrey—it sort of just happened. But our relationship coming to be was another story. It required traveling a long distance and navigating some tough terrain—valleys of uncertainty and mountains of doubt. That's the road of the patient pursuit.

AUDREY

I changed my outfit three times that morning. But I wasn't deciding between dresses and jewelry; I was deciding between mud clothes and hiking boots. I had no idea what to wear for the occasion, but I wasn't about to be the rookie suburban girl who asked. The sun was barely beaming through the blinds in my bedroom window when Zach's Subaru Outback full of country boys pulled up to my parents' house. In addition to Zach, the crew included Jeremy, Mueller, Roth, and Jake.

Jeremy got out of the car and came to my door. Whether he was picking me up or dropping me off, he *always* came to the door. I wasn't used to that in a guy, but I respected him for it. After joining the rest of the boys in the car, I was told we had one more stop to make on our way. We were picking up Tori, Zach's new girlfriend. *Relief!* I wouldn't be the only girl on this adventure.

After a few hours of listening to country music, reminiscing about past summer excursions, and dreaming up future ones, we reached our destination—Ape Cave.[1] Ape Cave is the longest continuous lava tube in the continental United States, and the third longest (in total mapped length) in North America. The tunnel runs 2.5 miles underground just north of Mount St. Helens in Washington State.

Ape Cave is sometimes referred to as Ape Caves (plural) because the main entrance falls between the lava tube's two ends, the Lower Cave and the Upper Cave. The Upper Cave is a 2.8-mile hike round-trip. First, there is a 1.5-mile descent on slippery, dark, rocky terrain in an underground tunnel. The tunnel eventually leads to a ladder that ascends to an opening in the cave's ceiling, the exit. The return hike follows a 1.3-mile trail that winds through the forest back to the main entrance. The Lower Cave is just a 1.5-mile hike round-trip and is considerably easier. The terrain is flat, broad, and covered with sand and mud rather than loose rock. As we piled out of the car and walked toward the main entrance, it wasn't even a consideration. We headed straight for the Upper Cave.

We immediately encountered terrain that demanded both agility and caution—well, for me at least. The boys, on the other hand, took off like Super Mario Bros. I could hear the iconic theme song playing in my head as I watched them bounce over the rocks full steam ahead. For them, this was beginner-level stuff.

I was torn between wanting to impress Jeremy by bounding ahead and not wanting to get myself in trouble. I wasn't afraid or uncoordinated, but I was cautious. Unlike the rest of the gang, I had a little more at stake if I got injured. If I slid on a rock or twisted an ankle, my collegiate running career could be on the line. So I methodically wobbled my way into the darkness, hunched over, sometimes on all fours, much more apelike.

As we progressed deeper into the cave, it grew colder and darker until Jeremy finally struck a match and lit the lantern. Something about this scene ignited a spark in me, or maybe I just have a thing for lanterns. I'd never seen a real old-school lantern fired up before. Boys from my high school didn't own this kind of stuff. But I loved that Jeremy brought the lantern instead of a flashlight. He was prepared, but in a nonconventional kind of way. It made our whole adventure feel more enchanting. The light from the lantern bounced off the walls of the cave. It was an absolute necessity for our journey onward.

We hiked a little farther and then decided to turn off the lantern to see how dark it really was. I'd never experienced such utter darkness with my eyes open. Blind to everything around us, we walked around like mummies with outstretched arms until we bumped into each other. Jeremy and I connected for a moment. I knew it was him because I felt the lantern brush past my leg. It was one of the first times we'd touched each other. It lasted just a split second, but even in the dark I felt the chemistry between us building. *What if he kisses me? No one would know, and we wouldn't even be able to see each other's reaction!* Jeremy was unpredictable and charming—it seemed like something he would do, which made me incredibly nervous. I was interested in Jeremy, but I definitely wasn't ready for that.

This was one of many "kissable moments" we would have over the next year and a half of being *just friends*. They all would have made for epic first-kiss stories, but we refrained. The full extent of our physical connection in those years was limited to bumping into each other in Ape Cave, sitting shoulder to shoulder in the back of the truck, and high fiving after our Fugitive victory. Even when we side-hugged good-bye, we were sure to leave room for the Holy Spirit. You might be chuckling now, but we'll talk about how we messed up in later chapters. However, I think if we had jumped directly into a dating relationship, we would have been tempted to flirt with sexual intimacy much sooner. Instead, for the two years before we officially dated, we hardly touched each other.

Jeremy relit the lantern, and we eventually reached the end of the tunnel with no significant injuries. We ascended the ladder and greeted daylight like newborns, squinting and stretching to adjust to the newly bright environment. As we hiked back to the car, Jeremy and I fell into an easy and meaningful conversation.

This was how our adventures often unfolded. In the thick of it, we were focused on fully enjoying the moment. Afterward, the adrenaline rush fueled honest, refreshing, and meaningful conversations. We learned so much about each other through our adventures and the conversations that followed. Whether it was geocaching, going to drive-in movies, bike riding, or cruising around in Jer's vintage orange BMW until we got lost, every adventure was an opportunity to discover more of each other's character. We both knew that strong relationships come from strong friendships, so we continued to build the foundation of our friendship.

For me, it was also a chance to watch for any potential red flags. It prevented me from falling into the blind-love trap—hurrying into a relationship, dabbling with sexual intimacy, and becoming emotionally attached. You know, like when the person you're dating becomes "the most talented, most interesting, and most extraordinary person in the universe." (And if that line doesn't sound familiar, please go watch *The Lego Movie* after you finish this chapter. It's sure to solve all of your dating problems.) As time passes, your friends and family might start to raise concerns about this most extraordinary person you're dating, but you won't listen because you literally can't see what they see. This is a titanic problem. One of the key ingredients to a healthy relationship is generous servings of input from the people who love and care about you.

Additionally, I didn't want to spend too much time with a guy I couldn't see a future with. Ultimately, what's the point of dating if not to find your spouse? In the words of novelist Nicholas Sparks, "I mean, if the relationship can't survive the long term, why on earth would it be worth my time and energy for the short term?"[2] Falling in love with someone you don't see a future with always ends with broken hearts. As I watched a close friend experience this heartbreak, I sensed the Lord warning me, *You can't help who you fall in love with, but you can help who you spend time with.*

* * *

If you're single and searching for a lifelong soul mate, *search for a friend*. We have all had that friend—maybe it's you—who met someone they were attracted to and started dating five days later. A few months pass, and the relationship crumbles. Why? Because there was no foundation and no infrastructure to build on. Dating before becoming friends is like trying to make a sandwich by starting with condiments rather than bread. It's messy, and it just doesn't work. You have to lay down the bread first. Then the condiments have something to stick to, and there's a foundation for the meat and cheese. Okay, I realize that may not be the most profound analogy, but you get the idea.

A longing for friendship and relational connection is hardwired into our DNA. Friendship is not a means to an end, but a key ingredient for meeting our innate human needs for relational connection. I think that's why so many couples say they married their best friend. It's much easier to add physical intimacy to friendship than it is to cultivate a strong friendship after having been physically intimate. That's one of the reasons Jeremy and I are such advocates for being friends first.

In our experience, friendship allows the groundwork for healthy pursuit to take place. To all the single women reading this, volume up! You're not giving a man the chance to pursue you if you're skipping the friendship space and jumping straight into getting physically intimate or chasing down every nice guy who looks your way. Not to mention, if you're the one doing *all* the chasing, chances are the guy you're after does not want to be caught, or *he's just not that into you*.

Friendship allows us time to find out if the person we're pursuing—or being pursued by—is marriage material before the relationship gets muddled with sexual intimacy. You'll find out if he's willing to risk rejection and is determined to be a thoughtful, faithful, and loyal friend. Our period of friendship gave Jeremy the opportunity to pursue me and gave us a strong foundation for when it was time to get physically intimate.

I also want to address a lie that may be creeping into your mind right about now: *There are no guys out there who will pursue me like that.* If you believe this lie, you'll live this lie. Jeremy is *not* an exception. Don't you believe it for a second. Of course, in my biased opinion I think he is a one-of-a-kind guy, but he's not an anomaly. It's like that classic quote often attributed to Henry Ford: "Whether you think you can or you think you can't, you're right." Whether you think you'll never find a godly, romantic, handsome guy or you think you will, you're right.

The friends-first approach also gave Jeremy and me the freedom to get to know each other without being pressured by the dating label or the intoxicating fog of physical intimacy. Once you open the door to physical intimacy, you're increasingly compelled to move very fast in that direction. But what if you don't want to? What if you just want to get to know each other for a while? What if you want the next person you date—or the only person you date—to be your spouse?

Western culture puts too much sexual pressure on dating. And Christian culture often puts too much pressure on the idea of finding "the one." As a general rule, whenever pressure is present, there is a higher chance of an injury. I think that principle applies as equally to relationships as it does to hot water boiling on the stove or to an overinflated tire. Anything that's overpressurized is dangerous. When it comes to dating, patience deflates pressure.

There is a reason the best intimate relationships come from friendships. When the rush of those first electric feelings fade, as they inevitably do, you'll still be doing life with someone you enjoy. You'll have someone to laugh and adventure with. Someone who gets your inside jokes. You'll have a friend.

Starting as friends gave us the foundation we needed for a healthy dating relationship. It empowered Jer's pursuit, eliminated the pressure of the dating label, protected our purity, and kept us from being blinded by emotional euphoria. Our friendship gave way to the patient pursuit. Much like the lantern was a necessity to navigate our journey through Ape Cave, so our friendship was a necessity to navigate our journey to marriage. Much like the Milky Way lit our path to the clearing, our friendship glimmered bright with anticipation over what might be. Much like the campfire ignited meaningful conversations, friendship was the spark that ignited our love. The actor Bruce Lee wrote, "Love is like a friendship caught on fire, very pretty, often hot and fierce, but still only light and flickering. As love grows older our hearts mature, and our love becomes as coals deep-burning and unquenchable."[3]

2

NOT AN
Island

JEREMY

I was the guy who started dating a girl once and then got told by people that we weren't the best match—how dare they! Maybe it was because I began dressing emo, listening to bad music, and only wore black. They also pointed out that I acted like a different person around her. I was "gloomier" than usual. The disapproving and unaffirming remarks from our friends only caused us to isolate even more, which led to mistakes and some friendships that were stretched and strained.

Hindsight is twenty-twenty, and looking back, I would have dodged some heartache had I acknowledged the concerns and red flags raised by my close friends. What I learned was that if you isolate yourself in a dating relationship, chances are that it's not because of something good. Isolation can be a way of hiding. And do we ever hide unless there is something we're hiding from? Whatever the reason, isolation allows for unchecked behavior. It's a way to escape issues in our life or our relationships, and that's exactly what I did in this relationship. Admittedly, isolation and escape were also coping mechanisms I was quite familiar with in my life outside of dating, but more on that in a later chapter.

I wasn't about to make the same mistake with Audrey when we started hanging out, so instead of isolating, I was intentional about integrating. This time, I was met with green flags.

*　*　*

Five months after I first met Audrey and her friends, fifteen of us circled around a cereal bowl in her parents' living room. We were playing a game called "Loaded Questions." The bowl was filled with slips of paper, each one containing a scribbled answer to a question. The questions included things like, "How would you describe the perfect summer day?" "If you could travel anywhere in the world where would you go?" "If you could have dinner with anyone in the world, dead or alive, who would it be?" Once everyone had dropped their answers into the bowl, one person read all the answers out loud. Then the rest of us tried to guess who had written each one.

Audrey and I ended up writing down the exact same answers that night—twice! Our answers to the *perfect summer day* question included camping by a lake, and we both said that we would travel to Switzerland! The fact that our answers were the same was a complete shock to everyone because it pretty much never happens in this game. Our friends laughed about it because it just affirmed what they already saw in Audrey and me—that we were kindred spirits. This was just a game, but it became one of the many affirmations we were beginning to notice.

You'd think that after enough incidences such as this one, Audrey would have started expressing her feelings for me—but nope! It was obvious I wasn't going to break through Audrey's walls by beating at the door. The only way I was ever going to win her heart was if she opened the door from the inside. Looking back, this worked in our favor because it forced my patient pursuit, which in turn gave us plenty of time to vet one another through our friends.

Audrey and I included our families in our relationship as well. We wanted to give them the opportunity to raise red flags too. Not long after meeting Audrey, I walked into the kitchen where my mom was making homemade granola and proclaimed, "Mom, I'm going to marry this girl." At this point, we had only seen each other a few times and it was still several months before we would spend our first summer together.

My mom chuckled as she placed a sheet pan in the oven, but when she turned back around to face me, she saw the look on my face and realized I was serious. Removing her mittens, she told me she thought Audrey was "very nice" and that she seemed like "your kind of girl." Although Audrey didn't spend as much time with my family as I did with hers, my parents still liked her spunk and respected her, based on what I had told them about her.

In addition to our parents and friends, we spent time with each other's siblings. That Thanksgiving, I coaxed my brothers and sister into stopping by the Bottis after our annual Roloff indoor soccer game. I'm not sure why they agreed to come, but next thing you know, there we all were, hanging out in the Bottis' living room playing the infamous "Loaded Questions" game. Afterward, I asked Zach, Molly, and Jacob what they thought of Audrey. They loved her and her family. It was affirming that the most trusted people in my life respected and encouraged my relationship with Audrey.

I don't mean for this to be prescriptive at all, but we even had strangers who affirmed our relationship. Once when I was visiting Audrey at school in Corvallis, we hit up the Broken Yolk Cafe for what we thought would be a quick breakfast before I made the ninety-minute drive north back to Portland. We weren't officially dating yet, but we had a "no phone" rule we adhered to during meals that kept us present and attentive to each other—so much so that we hadn't noticed we'd talked an hour past closing time! We were the last ones seated in the restaurant, and most of the staff had already gone home. Shocked, we waved down our waitress who was still cleaning up, and she brought us our check. When we apologized, she assured us it was no problem. "I could feel the love between you guys," she said, "and I didn't want it to end." We smiled and took the compliment. Neither of us had the heart to tell her, *Oh, we're just friends.*

We continued to see each other on occasional weekends throughout the winter and spring, but once Audrey was home for summer break, we started hanging out all the time again. This would be our second summer together as just friends—learning more about each other and each other's friends.

The summer was a mix of routine meetups and spontaneous adventures. We spent most Sunday evenings at church with friends and usually went to Audrey's parents' house to slam some pancakes. There were trips to nearby lakes and rivers, where we boated, swam, and explored in hopes of finding a rope swing. And, of course, there were the late-night hangouts with everyone by the campfire at the farm where we were serenaded by the soothing crackle of the fire as we talked late into the night. Audrey and

I typically sat across the firepit from each other, and I sometimes peered at her through the sparks, waiting for her to notice. She rarely obliged, but then again, neither did I—yet we both knew we did it, even if it was just for a second. Hasn't everyone had a time when they kept looking at their crush but wouldn't dare get caught doing it? We lingered by the fire after the last of our friends had jumped on the mule and headed back to the farmhouse. Sometimes we sat together in silence; sometimes we shared stories and aspirations.

I have especially vivid memories of the last night we were together before I left for Santa Barbara. Friends and family had all gathered to bid me farewell. Nine days before, Audrey and I had thrown our shoes over the train trestle to timestamp our summer and mark the decision that we were now officially dating. A night around the campfire was the one thing I wanted to do before I left. Amid the laughter, reminiscing and good-byes, I slipped away into the field for a minute to look back and take it all in. I wanted to remember the scene that grew our love story. As I looked back, excitement and fear were all wrapped up into one moment. I was about to embark on a new chapter.

I turned back around to look up at the night sky while I listened to the hum of conversation behind me. Moments later, my friend Dan, whom I've known since childhood, put his hand on my shoulder. "This is the best version of you that I've seen," he said. "Don't lose her." The words were spoken by Dan, but I knew all of my friends would have said the same thing— everyone recognized that I had something special with Audrey. Little did I know that it would be the affirmation of these same friends that would help Audrey and me endure the trials we would soon face.

AUDREY

One of the first things Jeremy and I bonded over was our unashamed desire to be unique and to live creative lives. Our friends often teased us both for our quirky idiosyncrasies. Because we spent so much time with each other's friends, I witnessed the eye rolls and astonished looks Jeremy's friends made when he wore his skin-tight jeans (this was before skinny jeans were a thing) or when he stood a little too close to the edge of the train trestle or when he drove off-road and narrowly escaped crashing the mule. Likewise, he witnessed my friends poking fun at my tomboy wardrobe, my affinity for McDonald's, and my ignorance of pop culture and celebrity gossip. But all of this teasing only intensified our intrigue for each other.

The first winter break after we were dating, all of my best friends and their significant others planned a weekend snow trip to Black Butte Ranch, a resort community where one of my friend's parents had a vacation home. Among the gang were Kelcey and Mitch, the friends who had set us up on our initial blind date. It would be the first time my friends spent more than a few hours around Jeremy, so I was eager to hear what they thought after spending some concentrated time with him. These were trusted friends, so I valued their opinion. We all arrived and claimed our bunks—girls in the upstairs rooms and guys in the downstairs rooms. And yes, we actually slept separately. I was thankful to have friends who also valued purity.

It was the weekend before Christmas, and we had planned some festive activities, one of which was a gingerbread house competition. After settling in, we made a group trip into town for supplies. Each couple had ten minutes to wander the aisles at Safeway and gather materials for their gingerbread house. Jeremy and I instantly knew we didn't want to use all the cliché materials—candy canes, marsh-mallows, gumdrops. So we stocked up on pretzels, animal crackers, and birthday candles. Secretly making our way through the check-out line, we kept our supplies concealed from the other couples.

Back at the house, the competition began, each of us in a secluded corner to protect our building process from copycat infringement. Jeremy and I were lucky enough to claim prime construction-site real estate at the kitchen table. We agreed that everyone would have thirty minutes to construct and decorate. Then we would vote for the best house, but you couldn't vote for your own.

Jeremy and I began by laying down a thick base of frosting and then sinking in graham crackers for a wraparound porch. The house was a 1920s farmhouse with a huge deck featuring Oreo lawn chairs and a banana peel slide coming down off the roof. The yard featured a lush spread of green sprinkles with animal cracker sheep wandering about. On the edge of the property was a campfire pit constructed with pretzel logs and some birthday candles at the center. Slices of banana circled the pit for seating. A peanut butter path framed by lettuce shrubs paved the way to the front door. I'm not sure why we went for the red licorice swirl look on the roof.

Moments before the big reveal, Jeremy lit the birthday candles we had installed in the firepit and the chimney. Our house was sure to win—it was literally "lit"! While we admired our ingenuity with pride, the rest of our friends just laughed. It was attention-grabbing for sure, but not because of its beauty or symmetry. We didn't win "best overall," but we killed it in the "most creative" category. And that's exactly how it was with our love story. It was far from perfect, but it was inviting, creative, and on fire.

Our Black Butte getaway gave our friends the opportunities to affirm, or advise against, our relationship. We were adamant about integrating rather than isolating. At the end of the trip, it was clear that my friends approved of Jeremy. They found it both comical and shocking that I found someone whose mannerisms complemented my quirks and whose personality matched my intensity.

JEREMY

Audrey had some stubborn walls, so in order to get her to look my direction, I had to get to know her friends and family. I think this was Audrey's way of luring me in for approval. Both Audrey and I were intentional about introducing each other to our friends and family and then later consulting their opinions. And honestly, I think we were both excited to introduce each other. It was like we were proud of each other and wanted to show each other off rather than keeping our relationship private in the fear that people would raise red flags. With Audrey, it was green flags all around.

I understand that this will not be the case for everyone. Finding trustworthy friends can be difficult. Dan happened to be a friend I grew up with. He helped steer me away from the wrong girls—even when I wouldn't listen—and put an affirming hand on my shoulder when the right girl came along. He had become someone I trusted and could go to for counsel.

One of my favorite Scripture verses speaks directly to the importance of having other people involved in our life. "Where there is no counsel, the people fall; but in the multitude of counselors there is safety" (Proverbs 11:14 NKJV). Whatever stage you are at in your relationship, take a minute and think about your community. Are you giving them an opportunity to either laugh in affirmation or raise a red flag of concern? Are you allowing them to put a hand on your shoulder to signal approval or caution? Are you giving your friends and your family a chance to pipe in? This doesn't happen when we treat ourselves or our relationships like an island.

You may be thinking, *Okay, Jer, I'm not in a relationship, so . . .* Regardless, we all have the opportunity to *be* wise counsel. Sometimes it means playing the role of an affirmer; sometimes it means raising red flags. Is there a couple in your life you deeply respect and look up to but you've never told them how much you admire their love? Maybe you have the opportunity to be the affirming hand on the shoulder. May I challenge you to text or call them when you finish this chapter?

On the contrary, do you have any friends who are currently in toxic or unhealthy relationships? Maybe you have a friend who suddenly became really isolating when they started dating someone new? Maybe God is pressing you to be the courageous and compassionate truth-teller. Speaking truth in love is a delicate balance. It's hard to be the one raising a red flag, but it just may be the most gracious and loving thing you can do for your friend. It's much harder to watch your friends get hurt, knowing that your warning might have helped prevent their heartbreak.

If our trusted allies had expressed serious concerns, I doubt our relationship would have endured very long. As Audrey noted in the previous chapter, emotions are beautiful, but they can also blind us. We can get lost in the fog of feeling. When that intoxicating fog rolls in, friends are our lighthouse on the shore, shining a beaming light of clarity to help us navigate safe passage.

3

EVERY WALL
Must Fall

AUDREY

I was a bit of a tomboy in high school. I dressed like one, acted like one, competed like one, and dated like one. I was *not* the girl who always had a boyfriend. Dating was fun, but that was about it. I enjoyed learning to drive a stick shift, took advantage of free ice cream, and liked going to the fair and watching movies, but beyond that, I didn't see a point in dating. I wasn't ready for marriage, so I was wary of prematurely getting caught up in a serious dating relationship.

I had a few short-term boyfriends in my early high school days, but we high fived more than we hugged. And like clockwork, two months in, I had a pattern of breaking it off over text messages. Usually because he wanted to hang out more or get physical, and I wasn't willing to sacrifice spending time with my friends, family, and teammates to make out on the couch. After each breakup, I felt a sense of freedom and relief. I didn't like feeling like I had to report to anyone. I probably came across as uninviting, cold, and intimidating to most guys. It was going to take a lot for me to surrender my treasured independence, so I blocked any potential boyfriends with a wall of rejection.

Before Jeremy, I had only one serious boyfriend. We dated for two years, beginning toward the end of my junior year of high school. In Christian circles it was what is sometimes referred to as the classic "missionary" dating story. It started out as my wanting to lead him to Jesus and then coming to realize the unhealthy ramifications of that mission. Throughout the course of our relationship, my boyfriend started following Jesus, which I was so excited about. He went to church and respected my faith, but as our relationship progressed, I began to question it. I was always the one fighting for purity, pushing for church, or sending him Scripture or books to read. He was a great guy, but I began to wonder if he was pursuing Jesus to get to me. In hindsight, it was as if he was putting me on the throne of his life rather than Christ, which is a mayday signal for any relationship.

Amid the emotional ecstasy of falling in love, it can be easy to glorify our earthly love story over God's eternal love story, exalting the love of our life over the Lord of our life. God designed us to worship him and no one else before or in place of him. But this doesn't mean our love for God takes away from our love for others. Absolutely not! It's actually the opposite. As we seek to love and worship Christ more, we are able to more creatively, more patiently, more selflessly, and more unconditionally love others. The best way to love your boyfriend, girlfriend, or spouse is to love God first.

Let's say the person you're dating right now doesn't share the same love of Jesus and commitment to the Word of God that you have. Let's say you think they have potential to be a future spouse, so you disregard your differences in faith. If that's true of your relationship right now, would the person you're dating continue to pursue Jesus passionately and faithfully if you broke up tomorrow? Would you?

Needless to say, I ran into some red flags with this boyfriend, especially as we wrestled with physical boundaries. I was in the business of waiting until marriage. Out of respect for me, he never pressured me to be physically intimate, but he never took the lead in fighting for purity either. Because we didn't share the same commitment to our faith, we didn't share the same commitment to purity. So we flirted with the line, which left me feeling ashamed and guilty and left him wanting even more. Turns out, it's a lot easier to get pulled down than it is to pull someone up. It's basic physics. Think about it.

Long story short, after months of struggling and becoming more aware of the differences in commitment to our faith, the Holy Spirit sucker punched me. I knew that ignoring my convictions meant sinning against my own conscience (James 4:17). I also knew I wanted a husband who would be a spiritual leader (Ephesians 5:22–23), and that was not the case in my current relationship. Although I was conflicted, I felt strongly that I should break up with him. Sometimes good is the enemy of best, and although what I had with my boyfriend at the time was good, it was keeping me from experiencing God's best—a relationship centered on Christ, and a man who loved God more than he loved me. I also sensed that the Lord was inviting me to trust him in the breakup. I felt like it was a testing of my faith, and I was reminded to surrender my love story to his faithful authorship.

At this point, we were both freshmen in college and attended schools a few hours away from each other, so I waited to end it until we were home from college during winter break. Unlike my previous breakups, this time I didn't feel freedom and relief afterward. I cried brokenhearted tears and felt overcome by doubts and questions.

Will my aching heart ever heal? Are my standards just too high? We had so many of the same friends—would one of us stop getting invited to things? Will I ever find a guy who loves Jesus as much as I do?

It was hard and it hurt, but I soon felt confirmed that it was the right decision. I was so blessed by the time of singleness that followed. I know this may seem like a Christian cliché, but I really did sense that God was encouraging me to be more focused on becoming a godly woman than on finding a godly man. So I shifted my focus to searching my own heart rather than searching for someone else's.

God has a sense of humor, because one week after I broke things off with my boyfriend, my friend Mitch, who was dating my friend Kelcey, texted me and invited me to go on a double date with one of his high school soccer friends. *Are you kidding? I've never been set up on a blind date before, and no way am I ready to start dating again.* My heart was barricaded with windowless cement walls that weren't ready to come down anytime soon. My gut reaction was to immediately turn down the invite, but something pushed me to say yes—and so did my friends. I trusted that Kelcey and Mitch wouldn't make it weird, knowing that I was fresh off a breakup.

In case you didn't see this coming, that was the night I met Jeremy.

I firmly believe if I had delayed the breakup conversation even one more week, I would have never met Jeremy. I would have returned to school and missed my chance. It was only when I chose to trust Jesus in the breakup—to risk temporary heartache in order to walk in his will—that I was free to meet my future husband. Needless to say, when I met Jeremy, I was still guarded, and the walls I had put up would require some time and trust before tumbling down.

* * *

August 1, 2011, was a turning point in our love story. It marked the beginning of more than friendship and the breaking down of some of my stubborn walls. Jeremy and I met up for our late-afternoon ten-miler. I was the team captain of my cross-country and track team, so running fifty miles a week was my summer job. Conveniently, Jeremy's summer job was working to win my heart. He rode his bike next to me while I spent hours in the blazing heat pounding the pavement and traversing the Portland hills.

Our routine "run and ride," as we coined it, became the prelude to our evening adventures. If we talked while en route, it was usually about the previous week's message at church, the books we were reading, our dreams of traveling, or our summer bucket list. We never talked about Jeremy moving to California at the end of the summer, although it was always there in the back of our minds.

On this particular run, we were nostalgically reviewing all the things we had crossed off our summer bucket list. There was only one thing left on the list that we both agreed we had to do—walk across the train trestle. With a height of ninety feet and a span of 1,168 feet, it is the largest wooden bridge in the United States still in use. The train tracks run right through Roloff Farms, and the trestle bridge is just a half-mile walk away.

When we returned from our run and ride, we quickly threw some clean clothes on our sweaty bodies, grabbed some snacks from the Roloffs' refrigerator, and set off walking along the wooden planks between the track's iron rails.

When we reached the beginning of the bridge, Jeremy did not break stride. He walked across the planks as if there was solid ground beneath his feet. I nervously followed behind, trying to mask my apprehension with a confident and fearless demeanor. With each step, the ground beneath us dropped lower. I'm not afraid of heights, but in this situation, you don't really have the option to not look down. I kept my eyes glued to the trestle beams as I carefully placed one foot in front of the other.

At the highest point of the bridge, we stopped to sit down and take in the beauty of the golden hour in Helvetia. I felt surprisingly calm, given the elements of danger we were exposed to. I always felt safe when I was with Jeremy. He was a daredevil, but he wasn't reckless. He was confident, but not in a cocky way. He was calculated and aware. My trust in his discernment was one of the things that eventually helped break down my relational fears and insecurities.

We sat in the middle of the trestle for a little while and talked. It was a welcome respite for my shaky legs. When our conversation slowed, Jeremy stood up without warning and took a step out over the edge of the trestle. I froze in both astonishment and fear. I may have even peed a little. Miraculously, he didn't fall. It was some kind of a Tom Sawyer stunt. He had simply stepped out onto the lip of one of the supporting crossbeams that run under the bridge. Still standing over the edge, he glanced back at me with a smirk and a slightly raised eyebrow. I loosened my grip on the rail line and smirked back. We had an undeniable connection or chemistry or vibe—or whatever it is the kids call it these days.

Jeremy pointed to the other side of the bridge and took off, bounding across the beams. I vigilantly followed him. The whole scene was straight out of *Stand by Me*, except we weren't searching for a dead body and there wasn't a train chasing us. Instead, we were both searching for some subtle way to confess our affection. We were nervous because we knew that to do so meant putting our friendship at risk.

When we reached the other side of the bridge, Jeremy pulled out his harmonica and started to play. That summer, we discovered that we both wanted to learn to play the harmonica, so I had mine in my backpack too. I pulled it out and joined him in the melody. We attempted to play a bluesy "Amazing Grace" while continuing to walk down the tracks. Maybe you're grimacing at how quirky this might seem, but for us it didn't seem cheesy or weird. It was refreshing to be with someone who complemented my nonconformity rather than someone who poked fun at my silly aspirations.

After a few minutes of practicing our new hobby, we heard howling in the distance. Our jaws dropped, and we looked at each other with bewildered joy. The coyotes were harmonizing with us! We stood still and reveled in their response, our faces brimming with wonder. Then we continued to play, pausing every now and then to let the coyotes have their solo performance. It was a beautifully surreal moment.

We had been so captivated by our senses that we didn't realize how far down the tracks we had walked. Once we realized where we were, we turned around to head back. When we reached the bridge to cross it for the second time, Jeremy stopped and looked at me.

"This is the most romantic thing I've ever done with a girl," he said—and then he added, "Not to push the envelope . . ."

My response sort of just fell out of my mouth, "You can push the envelope." Then I immediately felt flustered by my own words. Ready or not, I had just taken the "do not enter" sign off my heart.

I looked up from the tracks at him. His face resembled the sun-warmed cherries we had picked on our run and ride. I could see the relief and excitement in his eyes. We exchanged flirtatious smiles and continued walking back across the trestle, intoxicated by the truth we had just spoken and the electric silence that followed.

Then Jeremy's phone rang. It was his dad calling for a reason I can't remember, but when he asked what Jeremy was up to and found out we were at the trestle, he said, "Oh, I'm on my way down there on the mule right now. I'm showing it to some friends who wanted to see it. Want a ride back?"

Jer looked over at me to see what I thought. I shrugged my shoulders to indicate I could go either way. "Yeah, brilliant!" he replied to his dad.

Still crossing back over the trestle, we soon saw the mule and Jer's dad and friends below us. We waved, and they signaled for us to hurry down. When we reached the end of the bridge, we left the tracks and blazed a trail through the tall grass littered with daisies all the way down the hill to the road. When we reached the bottom, Jer's dad took a photo of us that, although blurry, stirs vivid memories to this day. There we are, both of us holding our harmonicas, browned by three months of long days in the sun, Jeremy for some reason wearing science goggles on his head (he later said he thought it would be funny), and me holding a bouquet of daisies I had picked on our way down the hill. That photo marks the end of our "strictly friends" phase, and the beginning of the demolition days ahead. I had walls we would be demolishing for years to come—and, spoiler alert, so did Jeremy.

We jumped in the back of the mule, and on our way back to the farm, I made a daisy crown. To this day, Jeremy still calls me Daisy Braids.

* * *

A couple of weeks after I became Daisy Braids, we became boy-friend and girlfriend—August 25, 2011. As you remember from the beginning of this book, that's when we tossed our shoes up on the wire hidden beneath the trestle.

During those two weeks leading up to becoming boyfriend and girlfriend, Jeremy attempted to kiss me for the first time. Evidently, my permission to push the envelope gave him the confidence. The night after our trestle adventure, we were lying in the hayfield by the campfire pit looking up at the stars, and he reached over and grabbed my hand for the first time. We were silent and still, locking in the moment.

Then he propped himself up on his elbow. I could see it coming, and I was paralyzed by the butterflies raging in my stomach. Immediately, I thought, *I'm not going to kiss him; we aren't even dating!* He leaned in and waited for me to lean toward him, but instead I looked down, and he kissed my forehead to recover from his rejection.

After two years of friend-zoning, you might have thought I was finally ready to let myself be known, loved, and kissed—to let my walls fall down—but I wasn't. It even took me a few days after we started dating to finally give in to our first kiss. I'll let Jeremy have his moment to tell that story here.

JEREMY

The campfire had stopped burning, and the night chill began to signal it was time to head back to the house. Walking back through the woods, I spotted a break in the tree line where the moonlight was pouring through. My heart began to beat faster as we approached. I paused at the break in the trees and pulled her in for a hug. It was just bright enough to see her face, and we kissed. Nothing had ever felt so right—a deep love being realized through a simple yet profound kiss. I kissed her a few more times on our way back as we discussed with humor how it had taken us so long and laughed about my failed attempt that night in the hayfield under the stars.

* * *

After we both went back to school, we didn't see each other for a couple of months. Then Jeremy decided to drive home from California for a weekend in October to help work the pumpkin season at Roloff Farms. I was at school in Corvallis, which was on his way but also a thirteen-hour drive from Santa Barbara. He drove through the night so we could have a whole day together before he continued on to the farm.

We spent the day driving around Corvallis so I could show him all my favorite spots, and then we went to dinner. I lived in a big house just off campus with six of my teammates, so Jeremy crashed on our living room couch that night before making the drive north to the farm. We kissed good night and went to bed. A few minutes later, I heard footsteps creaking up our rickety stairs, followed by a gentle knock on my bedroom door.

"Auj, I just need one more kiss good night," he said as he tiptoed in.

So I got up and kissed him again, followed by a prolonged hug. Then he looked at me and said, "Audrey, I love you."

I couldn't move my lips and my body locked up. I wasn't ready to say the L-word yet, but I also didn't want him to think I *didn't* love him. I was torn, so I was silent. After an awkward pause, Jeremy said, "It's okay; you don't have to say anything back. I don't want you to if you're not ready, but I just needed to tell you."

Well, it turns out I wasn't ready, and I remained not ready for another full year. I know, I'm horrible. It was only a month or so later that I knew with certainty that I *did* love him, but I still wasn't ready to say the words out loud. I didn't want to say I love you until I was positive that whomever I said it to would be my future husband. Looking back, I can't believe he kept dating me, pursuing me, and loving me, even after a year of patiently waiting for me to let my walls down.

JEREMY

A couple of months later, I was home again for Thanksgiving break, and a bunch of us had plans to go to the annual Christmas tree lighting ceremony in downtown Portland. We all met at a coffee shop next to Pioneer Square, where the lighting took place. After getting our coffee—as true Portlanders do—we bundled up and began our trek to the square. That's when Audrey and one of her friends took off and left me hanging. It wasn't the first time she'd done something like this. In fact, it was becoming a routine, and I wasn't happy about it. We had been dating for several months at the time, and I thought this behavior would change when our relationship status did. But no.

I don't consider myself a needy person by any stretch, but I did have some expectations about how we would treat one another—one of which was not running off unannounced after I bought her coffee on a group date. To put it bluntly, it was just rude. Especially since we didn't have many chances to spend time together due to long distance.

Running off with her friends itself wasn't the issue—it was that it seemed as if she didn't want to let me know or communicate with me at all. She acted like she didn't care about me one bit. The problem was a lack of affection and an absence of emotional connection that kept her from seeing how disrespectful her behavior was. I was starting to feel more like an afterthought than her friend, much less her boyfriend.

No one wants to be called a stage-five clinger. Before Audrey and I started dating, and even in our dating relationship, we were both afraid of being perceived as needy. Neither of us wanted to burden the other with our wounds, hurts, and struggles. And we definitely didn't want to be perceived as high-maintenance or clingy. We wanted to be easy to love and fun to be with. I don't think we are the only ones here. Mustering up the courage to express your needs in a relationship is like asking someone to dance. The fear of rejection keeps our feet planted by the punch bowl. But if you want to find true love, you have to step out onto the dance floor.

There's nothing wrong with wanting to be lovable and fun—until it keeps you from being vulnerable and honest. Most people don't want to be labeled as needy in their relationship, whether you're dating or married. But the reality is, we all have relational needs, and everyone's relational needs look different because everyone gives and receives love differently. Failing to communicate our relational needs can eventually leave us feeling frustrated, bitter, or angry with our beloved. When I say "needs," don't misinterpret that to mean your beloved is responsible for satisfying all of your needs. That's impractical and unhealthy. What I'm saying is that it's healthy and helpful to be aware of the ways you feel most loved.

I knew I had a choice. I could either lower my expectations for Audrey's behavior or communicate my needs and hope she would be willing to change. The other option was to break up. It wasn't an option I wanted, but it wasn't off my radar either. Through our friendship and my pursuit, I had already learned that Audrey had some formidable walls around her heart. Now I was beginning to realize that simply changing the status of our relationship wasn't going to break them all down. I decided to confront her about it before I went back to school.

I knew Audrey was independent, which was something I liked about her. But now I was starting to see that something more than independence was going on, especially since this behavior hadn't started with me. I came to find out, through spending time with her friends, that Audrey had a reputation for lack of affection and acting like she didn't care. She was known for concealing her emotions, blowing off dates, and high fiving her previous boyfriends good-bye.

This wasn't mere independence; it was an emotional wall of self-protection and pride. Knowing this, I had to proceed with caution. I knew that if Audrey wasn't willing to give up some of her independence, we'd have big problems moving forward. It seemed only natural to me that a girl would want to hug her boyfriend good-bye—and I don't think I'm alone here! I decided the conversation would be worth the risk. And I knew that tough conversations are always better the sooner you have them. In the short term, they're scary, but they can save hurt and hardship in the long term.

I confronted Audrey about her behavior a few days after Thanksgiving. Being careful with my words, I began to engage. "Hey, babe, can we talk about what happened at the tree lighting?"

"What do you mean?" Audrey replied.

"When you just blew me off and disappeared with Ellen and didn't communicate where you were going. You just left me with all of your friends without saying good-bye. I'm bringing it up because this isn't the first time something like this has happened. I honestly feel disrespected when you do this."

This conversation terrified me, not just because it took vulnerability and would be poking a vulnerable spot in her, but what if this was something she refused to acknowledge?

"Wow, I am so sorry. I've been told my independent spirit can get the best of me sometimes." I was relieved at her response. She thanked me for my honesty and expressed her willingness to change.

To my surprise, this conversation initiated change in Audrey much more quickly than I had anticipated! She became more affectionate toward me and started sharing her emotions freely. It was as if a locked room in her heart had suddenly been flung wide open. I think being locked up behind such high walls had become painful for her. Authors and psychologists Henry Cloud and John Townsend wrote, "We change our behavior when the pain of staying the same becomes greater than the pain of changing."[1] Audrey was ready for change.

Looking back, we consider the Christmas tree lighting confrontation as a critical juncture in our relationship. It marked the beginning of a new era for us, and I can't stress enough how the foundation of our friendship gave me the understanding, confidence, and authority to go into that conversation trusting in the Lord for a hopeful outcome. This confrontation helped break down Audrey's walls, but I had a few walls of my own. Later in our relationship, the roles would be reversed, and Audrey would be the one confronting me.

AUDREY

By now, I'm assuming everyone on this planet has seen at least one episode of *Fixer Upper*, the popular home makeover show in which Chip and Joanna Gaines turn broken-down houses into gorgeous homes. One of the first things the Gaineses always seem to say when they step into a potential remodel is, "We'll open up this room by taking down this wall." A couple commercial breaks later, there's Chip with a sledgehammer, swinging away at the drywall.

It always amazes me that the homeowners mostly seem fine with this. Rarely does anyone disagree with the Gaines's vision of opening up space in their home. Even if they're nervous about what lies behind the walls or the potential issues they could run into, they trust that the end result will be worth the mess and uncertainty. They also know that Chip has the right tools and that he knows what he's doing. While some walls are load-bearing and require extra caution and reengineering to tear down, others are purely aesthetic. Chip never gets confused about the difference. Plus, even though they don't capture it on the show, permits are usually required before walls can be removed. Doing demolition well isn't a hack job. It requires knowledge, skill, tools, and permits.

Do you see where I'm going with this? When it comes to dating and intimate relationships, everyone starts out with some emotional walls. Some people have walls that are relatively easy to take down, and others have walls that require extra care and time-consuming permitting to remove. Most of us have a mix of both. Sooner or later, the person you're dating is going to come to you with a permit, and you will be faced with a choice—open yourself up for a remodel or continue hiding behind a wall that needs to be mended up, rewired, or repaired. Doing demolition on emotional walls isn't a hack job either. It requires vulnerability, honesty, and trust.

When you find someone worth pursuing or when someone you could see yourself marrying starts pursuing you, consider it a permit for a character remodel. Our culture will tell you that you shouldn't need to change for someone else. "You do you" is the motto of our day. But I wonder how many relationships fail because of an unwillingness to change. Shouldn't the person you love be a catalyst for change in your life?

Just to clarify, this remodel isn't about changing yourself to make the person you're dating like you more—which is what my first serious boyfriend tried to do. It's about changing yourself because the person you're dating makes you want to be a better version of yourself. That's what happens when someone you care about holds up a mirror to your life and you begin to see yourself through his or her eyes.

If you are just out of a relationship and trying to heal from heartbreak, you may feel spooked by all this talk about taking down walls. I get it. And just to be clear, walls aren't always bad. When walls take the form of healthy boundaries, they can be good and serve a useful purpose. Walls set a limit that can help you sort out your emotions, keep you from rushing into things, and guard your heart. But when walls morph into prison fences that you can't take down, even when you want to, they do more harm than good. They keep you from achieving the depths of love. They hold you back. They create confusion and misunderstanding instead of honesty and clarity.

So if you've been single for a while or you can't understand why your relationships never seem to deepen or last, it may be that your walls are a little too high. Notice I said *walls*, not *standards*. When Jeremy and I met, we both had some skyscraper-high walls. I totally understand the desire to guard your heart and take it slow when it comes to dating. But eventually, every wall must fall. If we want to be fully known and fully loved, we must be willing to pick up the sledgehammer.

4

A CREATIVE
Type of Love

JEREMY

The night I met Audrey, I drove home more slowly than usual, lost in deep thought. I felt caught between wonder and uncertainty as I tried to make sense of the girl I'd just met. By the time I pulled into the gravel driveway at the farm, I had replayed the night several times and was imagining what might lie ahead. The night we met changed my life—love always does. And from there, love did what it does best—it compelled me into a pursuit that was full of creativity, adventure, and sacrifice. As I mentioned earlier, *the pursuit was on!*

The first gift I ever made Audrey I gave to her at Christmas the year we met. Auj was home from university for the winter break, and I was finishing up my last class of the term at a local community college. We made plans to see each other, and I was eager to make her something special.

I didn't know what she might like, so I built something I knew *I* would like—a lamp made out of an old kerosene lantern. I'd always wanted one, and Audrey was my motivation to finally tackle the project. I drilled some holes, installed a socket for the lightbulb, and wired in the switch. To my delight, it worked! I thought it was awesome and I had a hunch she would too. On the underside of the base I wrote, "To Audrey from Jeremy. Christmas 2010. Jeremiah 10:23."

Walking up to Audrey's house, my palms began to sweat, and I suddenly felt like a weirdo. *This is embarrassing. I'm going to scare her away—and we had just become friends! And besides, this lamp is cool. Maybe I should just keep it.* I imagined what her mother might think. *Who is this weirdo you barely know who's suddenly giving you extravagant handmade gifts?*

The fear was real.

I turned back toward the car to put the gift in the trunk and save myself the humiliation. I had only taken a few steps when I stopped in the street. *What kind of story do I want? Do I want to tell the story of how I cowardly refrained from giving Audrey her first gift, or the story of how I heroically overcame doubt and gave Audrey one of her favorite gifts ever?* This inner monologue was all the courage I needed to turn back around, gift in hand, and walk through that big brick archway, jaw clenched and heart racing.

I pressed the doorbell with a sweaty fingertip. Almost immediately, the door opened, and there stood Audrey's dad. I walked in a bit awkwardly, holding the lamp behind my back, and headed straight to the kitchen, where I could hear Audrey and her mom talking.

I didn't waste a minute of time. I pulled out the unwrapped treasure from behind my back and said, "I made this for you. Merry

Christmas!" Audrey and her mom both looked at it blankly and then looked back at me.

"What do you mean you *made* it?" her mom said with a puzzled look on her face.

"I mean I made it," I said.

"What's the cord for?" Audrey asked.

"It's a lamp!" I said, laughing. "Let me show you." I plugged it in, and it lit up—and so did their faces. They were surprised—in a good way. Audrey loved it. I got the idea that nobody had ever made her something so "sophisticated" before. She said it was the coolest gift anyone had ever given her. I think Audrey would have loved it even if it had just been an old rusty lantern I found in one of the barns. She took it back to school with her and set it on the nightstand by her bed. Today it resides on a table in our entryway. I got to keep it after all.

Not long after, it was summertime, and I was still very much in the friend zone. Audrey had mentioned that she had always wanted a one-way sign. So one night I went to what my friends and I called "the sign yard." It was a place filled with construction junk, broken traffic cones, and the occasional road sign. After an hour of hunting, I found one. On the back, I inscribed a poem I'd written and then gave the sign to her just in time for her to take it back to school in the fall. I hoped it would remind her of me whenever she saw it. It was another winner in the creative gift category!

I pursued Audrey with unique gifts, but I also tried to be creative in other ways, such as planning trips, attending events, and creating adventures. Then there was the time I did something I never thought I'd ever do for a girl—I ran.

* * *

It was June in Helvetia. The Helvetia Half Marathon is one of the largest races in the state, and also what Helvetia is best known for—besides Roloff Farms and the local tavern. Event organizers were setting up traffic cones and blocking off roads to mark the route. People from all over the city were gearing up for the run, and Audrey was one of them. I was not a runner—but put me in a soccer game, and I could run until I yakked! At least in soccer there's a point to the running. Long-distance running just for the sake of running was not my thing, no thank you.

A few weeks earlier, Audrey had jokingly asked if I wanted to join her in the race. I thought long and hard about it for about half a second and then declined. But on the morning of the big race, I woke up earlier than usual with a distinct feeling in my gut. *If I do not go on this run, it will be something we missed out on. I will have chosen the mundane—a few extra hours of sleep—over the memory. I want to be with her, even if it means misery for thirteen miles.* Again I asked, *What kind of love story do I want?* And again the answer was clear.

I jumped out of bed and scavenged through the closest for a pair of running shoes. All I found was an old pair of indoor soccer shoes that were torn along the side. Throwing them back into the closet, I spotted my Vibram FiveFingers in the corner. *Yes!* If the name doesn't sound familiar, you may know them by sight—they're the embarrassingly ugly rubberized shoes that look like bare feet. I wiggled them on, grabbed a soccer jersey, and headed down to the starting point at Hillsboro Stadium in high hopes of finding Audrey.

I parked my car and joined a mob of more than three thousand runners, all of us trying to find the right place to line up. There were signs with numbers indicating estimated pace, and everyone was supposed to line up according to their running speed. Not knowing what I was doing, I decided to stand next to a sign marked "10M+," indicating a pace of just over ten minutes per mile. I scanned the crowd for Audrey. *I bet she'll be surprised to see me!*

Bang! The gun went off, and the race began. I took off, hoping I'd see her during the race. By a few miles in, I thought I was doing pretty well. It wasn't until I was approaching the halfway point that I realized there was no way I was going to see her. This was a morale killer. I considered hightailing it for my bed by cutting through the field to my left, as the farm lay just beyond it, but I didn't. *If I can't see her, maybe I can at least impress her by finishing.* For love, I trudged on. Somehow, despite running in Vibram FiveFingers and having never trained, I finished the race!

I was hobbling painfully back to my car when I heard someone call out my name. Sitting on the grass nearby were a few of Audrey's cross-country teammates. When I asked where Audrey was, they said she had already left. I found out they had started the race standing under the sub-seven-minute mile sign and finished in the top 1 percent. Audrey had finished seventh overall and taken first in her age bracket. We chatted for a few minutes before I said good-bye and continued hobbling to my car. I was glad that at least I now had witnesses who could verify my story of accomplishment.

Audrey had invited me to attend her sister's graduation party later that evening. Even though I didn't know anyone, I decided to go. I thought it would be a good chance to get to know her family, secretly hoping they would encourage Auj to date me. But of course, I was mostly there for Auj—and the food.

I told Auj the story of the race, and she was shocked! Laughing at my efforts, she fixed me up with a plate of Botti post-race miracle food for my recovery—juicy ribs, cheesy pasta, and homemade berry cobbler. On the one hand, running the race was pointless because I never did get to see Audrey. On the other hand, hearing her laugh and answering her questions about how I did it made it more than worthwhile. I mean, she had to be impressed, right? The half marathon became part of our story. To this day, we joke that I ran a half marathon just for her.

The rest of the summer, I swapped my Vibrams for a bicycle and rode alongside her while she trained for cross-country season. Sometimes my pursuit seemed pointless because of the walls Audrey had up. After finishing a long ride, she often just said good-bye and left. I would drive home wondering if I was wasting my time. But love is persistent, creative, and sometimes crazy. So I was determined to keep riding as long as she kept running.

After Audrey went back to school in the fall, we only saw each other when she came home on occasional weekends. As the winter break approached, I had already set my sights on our second summer together. I wanted it to be the summer I made Audrey fall in love with me. To lay the groundwork, I decided I needed to ask Auj out on an official date during the winter break. It had been almost a year since our blind date. I had been wanting to do this for a while, but I was worried it might scare her away. But after talking with her best friend about it, I deemed it a perfect time to do so. I wanted to change the expectations for our upcoming summer. As if it wasn't obvious enough already, I wanted her to know I was crazy about her.

After pacing the lawn for thirty minutes, I finally made the call. In a shaky voice, I nervously told her I wanted to take her out on an official date when she was home at break. I was so relieved when she said yes, but just as we were hanging up from our awkward conversation, I heard a bunch of girls burst out laughing. Evidently, I had called her while she was in the car with all her friends, and she conveniently neglected to mention she had me on speakerphone. I felt a twinge of embarrassment, but not for long. I was pretty sure the camaraderie of her friends had factored in my favor.

It felt like winter break took forever to arrive, but when it did, I was ready. Picking her up in OhSo, I took her for a long drive through the hills of Portland, eventually ending up at Pittock Mansion, a beautiful, historic house museum overlooking the city. The museum was closed, but after talking as we sat at a picnic table and then touring the gardens, we got back in the car and headed for Rock Creek Tavern, an old barn-turned-restaurant tucked away in the Helvetia countryside. Rock Creek always has a fire going in the big stone fireplace and smooth music playing that complements the dim lights and smoky atmosphere.

We sat in what they call the "dating booth" (yes, really) under the stairs. We had a great time, and our conversation was filled with laughter and plans for the upcoming summer. While we were finishing up our meal, an older couple walked by our table as they were leaving and said, "Thank you." When we asked what for, they smiled and said, "For being in love, and for not being on your phones." We were embarrassed because we were far from exchanging "I love you"s, but we never let on. I appreciated the couple saying that, because it gave Auj all the more reason to fall in love with me. Something inside me burned brighter when things like this happened, and I wanted to believe it was mutual. I was tending the embers of our relationship, and every affirmation felt like a dry cedar log being tossed onto the fire. We ended up staying another hour or so after we finished our meal, enjoying coffee and ice cream while dreaming up summer adventures. We were going to take full advantage of our limited days together, so we wrote down our summer bucket list in my leather Moleskine.

After winter break, Audrey went back to school, but there was no denying that we had both left a piece of our heart with the other. Throughout the winter and spring we saw each other a fair amount when Audrey came home from school for a weekend or when I visited my friend Scott in Corvallis—which was really code for visiting Audrey. We mostly hung out in group settings with each other's friends until Audrey was home for summer break. And you already know what happened next—our summer of timelessness. Just as I'd hoped, at the end of our second summer, I asked Audrey to be my girlfriend, and we threw our shoes at the train trestle.

Once we started dating long-distance, I knew my creative pursuit had to persist for our love to survive. And we both knew our relationship could not thrive on text messages and Skype calls alone. We needed more than that to bridge the gap of 900 miles! As the summer came to an end, we discussed how we'd do this. What would keep two lovers in love—especially at a distance? Our answer? Intentionality, creativity, and faithfulness.

Our story felt both effortless and intentional at the same time. Looking ahead, we wanted to continue our creative pursuit. We wouldn't succumb to laziness—we couldn't! That would indeed be the end of us. That's when we decided to write letters. What better way to be intentional than to reclaim the effortful and artful practice used by the romantics of old! Before leaving for my new home, I handed Audrey her first letter, with a posture of certainty that we would find a way through this.

Upon my arrival in Santa Barbara, the first thing I did was visit an antique store to buy a manual typewriter. I wanted to be able to both hand-type and handwrite letters to Audrey. The typewriter was hard to use, but it was an intentional choice. Every letter I typed represented an hour, sometimes more, of love I poured into it.

I believe that love shows up through its efforts—and I also believe Audrey felt it. We committed to writing letters because they felt real, romantic, and creative—and that was the kind of relationship we wanted. We were also looking ahead in our story, and we liked the idea of one day having a big wooden box full of letters to look back at.

One of the things I struggled with most when we were apart was not being able to share experiences with Audrey. In the evenings, I often went for walks around my neighborhood, where the air was filled with the lovely scent of night-blooming jasmine. It's a bushy plant with beautiful white flowers that open only at night when the air is warm. I loved how they glowed beneath the streetlights and danced to the ocean breeze. I tried to describe them to Audrey, but it wasn't the same as sharing the experience with her.

In an effort to creatively love her, one night I picked a bunch and tucked them into my next letter. She called me when she opened it and said they smelled even better than I had described them! The smell of night jasmine became one of her favorite smells. Audrey is all into the potions now (essential oils) and has made a roller she calls "night jasmine." Whenever I smell it on her, it always triggers waves of nostalgia.

Although Audrey had a traditional three-month summer break, my school terms continued through the summer, with eight-week sessions followed by two-week breaks. That summer, she got a job working at Anthropologie in downtown Portland. At the start of one of my two-week breaks, I was headed to Portland for some filming. My mom picked me up from the airport, and I convinced her to swing by Anthropologie on our way home—which was completely out of the way—so I could give Audrey a poem I'd written on the typewriter. When I arrived, Auj was on her break, so I gave the note to her manager and asked her to pass it along. I'd initially been disappointed but then decided that the way things worked out was even better. In addition to being more creative, I hoped it would leave her blushing at work and heighten her anticipation of getting home, where I would be waiting for her.

When I was back in Santa Barbara, I continued my efforts to find creative ways to express my love. Sometimes I called local shops in Corvallis and had chocolate or flowers delivered to her house. Other times, I asked her friends to do little favors for me, such as put a note from me in whatever book she was reading at the time.

Audrey was also intentional and creative in expressing her love for me. For one of my birthdays she made a surprise visit to Santa Barbara. She had my roommate James sneak out and pick her up from the airport. It must have been one in the morning when she jumped on my bed and yelled, "Surprise! Happy birthday!" James was standing there laughing as he filmed it. I don't wake up easily from sleep, so it took me a moment to realize I wasn't just dreaming. At first, all I could do was repeat a confused, "Audrey?" But when she hugged me and I smelled her perfume, I knew it was real.

I felt so loved in that moment. I knew how much effort and planning it must have taken for Audrey to get time away from school and track practice and to coordinate her stay in Santa Barbara—all without me knowing.

I was happy to forget school for a few days and explore Santa Barbara with Audrey. This wasn't her first visit, but there was always so much more I wanted to show her each time she came. We drove Blue Moon to the top of the Santa Ynez Mountains for a hike, ate at the iconic Cold Spring Tavern in the hills of Santa Barbara, and visited all of my favorite coffee shops. I taught her how to kick a soccer ball and walk a slackline. Sometimes we'd find a good spot at the beach to sit and read together while the crashing waves drowned out everything else. We longed to do even the simplest things side by side.

One time when we were taking an evening barefoot stroll on the beach, Audrey looked at me and said, "Wanna go in?"

"It's pretty cold," I said smiling back at her. But before I could weigh the pros and cons of soaking my attire in saltwater, she was already running for the waves. I took off after her, and the adrenaline rush kept us warm while the stars began to show. There was something about being with Audrey that made me feel free. And I could sense she felt the same with me. When we finally realized we were freezing, we raced back to the van and wrapped ourselves in beach towels. Audrey put on one of my flannels, and I took her to the only coffee shop in Santa Barbara that was open twenty-four hours. We got chai tea lattes and talked about how good it felt just to be together. We never took our time with one another for granted.

When Audrey returned to school after my birthday visit, I had a strong case of the PABS, an acronym coined by my roommate James that stood for "Post-Audrey Blues Syndrome." I was always a little down after having to say good-bye—especially if we didn't know when we were going to see each other next. Those were always the hardest good-byes, and this was one of those times. It was so much easier when we were together, but being apart forced us to continue seeking more creative ways to love each other.

Although the letters were a pillar to our success and creative pursuit, they were not what got us through. The intentionality and patience required to write, send, and wait for them kept us excited. But ultimately it was not the letters, but our creative pursuit and what that represented.

AUDREY

Jeremy and I spent three years relentlessly checking our mailboxes. I checked my mailbox like it was the refrigerator, opening it multiple times throughout the day in hopes of finding something that wasn't there the last time I checked. Whenever a letter was there, I felt like I was opening a Willy Wonka chocolate bar with the golden ticket—especially when the letter was one he'd written on his typewriter. I always read his letters multiple times. It took everything in me not to immediately call him to talk about whatever he had written, but I refrained. We wanted to keep some things in writing only, and we didn't want our phone conversations to dilute the content of our letters.

The anticipation and emotion wrapped up in our letter writing helped ease the pains of separation, especially when the letters included "extras." Jeremy often added poems, photos, scents from Santa Barbara, CDs with his favorite songs, and other small and thoughtful gifts that reminded him of me. I added photos, poems (although they were more comedic than serious), sprayed perfume on my letters, and sent small gifts that reminded me of him.

In addition to writing letters, we were constantly thinking of ways to connect and grow in our relationship. We read the same books and listened to the same podcasts so we'd have something to talk about besides what was happening in our days apart. Sometimes we did homework together on Skype. We trudged through our work, stopping every now and then to stare at each other with a longing that ached to our bones. We read books aloud—mostly by C. S. Lewis, Francis Chan, and Timothy Keller—and talked about them.

When it came to phone calls, we figured out early on that we felt more connected by less frequent and deeper conversations than by more frequent and surface-level conversations. Nightly calls to download our days were more frustrating than helpful. We were always distracted by homework, roommates, or cooking dinner, and we couldn't talk long enough to get a good read on each other's emotions. Then we hung up the phone with false assumptions about how the other person was feeling or what they meant by something that was said. My goodness, to this day we do not recommend dating long-distance. It is not for the faint of heart.

We accepted that it was actually better for us to go a few days without talking so we could set aside enough time to have a conversation that went beyond just recapping our days. We also made it a point to discuss specific topics during our Skype or phone calls. Sometimes we prayed for each other, planned out what we'd do the next time we were together, or discussed specific events from our pasts that had shaped us. We were determined to connect even when we felt so disconnected. We were determined to communicate despite our faces freezing on the screen or our calls getting dropped. We knew that persistently and creatively expressing our love would be vital to sustaining our relationship.

One year, Jeremy was going on a road trip to Utah with all of his friends, and it happened to fall over Valentine's Day. Even though we wouldn't be together, I still wanted to make him feel loved from afar. I decided to send him a giant kiss—metaphorically and literally. I made a batch of the infamous Botti Rice Krispies treats, but instead of spreading them out into a pan to cool, I dumped that sticky mess into a giant funnel. Then I used my hands to sculpt it into the shape of a Hershey's Kiss. Marveling at my cleverness, I painted it in chocolate and covered it with tinfoil. Then I globbed on my signature red lipstick and repeatedly kissed a white strip of paper. This would be the "kisses" label protruding from the top.

I wrote Jeremy a letter and wrapped everything up in a nice pink-and-red box. I texted one of his friends and got the address of the place where they would be staying, and then I shipped the box so it would arrive the same day they did. I couldn't wait for him to open it.

Jeremy FaceTimed me when he got the box so I could watch him open it. His reaction was exactly what I had hoped for! He said he felt so loved and valued when he received my gift. Later, he explained that the most meaningful part about the gift wasn't the giant Rice Krispies kiss, but the words of affirmation in my Valentine's card.

Believe it or not, I was actually surprised by how much Jeremy appreciated my encouragement. It just seemed like everyone was always complimenting or praising Jeremy for something—his vintage cars, his soccer skills, the things he built, his photography, or something he did or said on TV. Not to mention that all the affirming comments people made on his social media posts were like Red Robin French fries—bottomless! I figured hearing similar compliments from me probably wouldn't mean much to him. I was wrong. Receiving words of encouragement and affirmation from the girl he loved meant more than thousands of compliments from strangers. For Jeremy, a card full of affirmations spoke more "I love you"s than a gift.

As we sought to love each other in more creative and meaningful ways, I suggested we take the love languages test. Both Jeremy and I were familiar with Gary Chapman's book *The Five Love Languages*, but neither of us had ever taken the test to determine what our own love languages might be.[1]

The five love languages are:

- words of affirmation
- quality time
- receiving gifts
- acts of service
- physical touch

Of course, most of us appreciate receiving love in all five ways, but the test helps to identify our primary love language. Then it describes what it means and suggests how we can use it to connect with others.

We took the test while on the phone together and then discussed our results. My top two love languages were tied between quality time and receiving gifts. Jeremy's top two love languages were tied between words of affirmation and physical touch.

As we processed our results, we gleaned insights on how to love each other in more creative and specific ways. It changed the way we expressed our love and helped us understand one another better. I became more intentional about deluging Jeremy with affirmation and also about holding his hand and never forgetting to hug good-bye. Jeremy learned how cherished I felt by all of his handmade gifts and surprise letters. He also learned how much I valued spending intentional quality time with him.

Through the love languages test and our discussion of it, we also learned the importance of staying curious about each other. We agreed that no matter how long we had been together, there would always be more we could learn about each other—our likes, our pasts, our day-to-day experiences, our struggles, our triumphs, our fears, our hopes and dreams. We knew this would become increasingly important as our relationship progressed because we would inevitably change and grow over the years. This reality excited us and spurred us on in our never-ending study of each other.

First Peter 3:7 (ESV) reads, "Husbands, live with your wives in an understanding way." First of all I don't think there's a woman on the planet who doesn't want the man she loves to understand her. Secondly, misunderstanding so often leads to strife in relationships. I realize that this specific Scripture is addressing husbands, but I think it's safe to say that this would be wise practice for wives too. One of the ways we love one another is by seeking to understand one another. We must be willing to keep learning more about the person we love. We must be students of one another—always extending grace, asking questions, and staying curious. *The Five Love Languages* became our cheat sheet for loving each other creatively and specifically.

JEREMY

One of the best gifts Audrey has ever given me happened in the first year we were married. It started out as a creative idea and ended up giving me far more than she ever could have imagined. Audrey thought it would be fun to give me something different for my birthday. Instead of a tangible gift, she gave me a relationship. I had been following an entrepreneur online for a while, and she knew I admired his writings and work. So she reached out to mutual friends and scheduled a meeting with him.

Auj convinced me we were going paragliding, but first we'd go out to lunch. As we walked up to the restaurant, a man approached me. Recognizing him, I said "Dale?"

"Jeremy, it's nice to meet you," he said.

Shocked and confused I looked over at Auj, who belted out a big, "Surprise!" We spent the afternoon talking about Jesus, biblical living, and our cultural moment. I drove home that day feeling encouraged, challenged, and curious about the things we had talked about. Audrey had no idea her gift would one day turn into a mentor and a great friend—truly her gift turned into more than she could have imagined.

During the first year of our marriage, we were living in Los Angeles, and Audrey had a laborious job that required her to wake up at 2:45 a.m. every day. Yes, you read that correctly. Commuting halfway across LA—which is a job in and of itself—she had to convince grumpy store managers to buy her company's product—wine. This job drained her, both emotionally and physically. Audrey was burned-out.

Knowing her love language, I knew she needed to get out of the routine for a minute, have fun, and spend some quality alone time—just the two of us. When she got home, I had a route all picked out and the motorcycle loaded up with our running gear. When she saw it, she gave a tired smile and dropped her shoulders in relief. We rode the Fox—our Honda CB360T motorcycle—up Laurel Canyon Boulevard and over to Mulholland Drive as we leisurely found our way to the Hollywood Reservoir—a place Auj had never been to. We ran a lap around and went out for ice cream afterward. On the ride back, I noticed she was hugging me extra tight.

Creative love requires thoughtfulness, and we believe—from experience—that the effort is totally worth it! We all have a creative side and a love story that is waiting to find its best expression. God the Creator made you and me in his image (Genesis 1:27; Isaiah 64:8). That means we have divine creative juices hardwired into our very DNA. The simple fact that no two human beings look or act the same is overwhelmingly magnificent and immensely creative. It's proof that you—yes, *you*—are creative and that your love story can be creative too. Auj and I believe that pursuing a creative love story is one of the best ways to put the love of Christ on display. Every time you express your love in a meaningful and creative way, you can confidently say, "There's more where that came from!" because God's power at work in us is able to do "immeasurably more than all we ask or imagine" (Ephesians 3:20).

All this to say, figure out your love languages, surprise each other, swim in the ocean, make thoughtful gifts, do something spontaneous, get a babysitter, get out from behind your phones, and get creative. Pursue a love that tells a story. Whether you are currently single and in pursuit, dating and falling in love, engaged and preparing for marriage, or married and protecting your promise, you have a unique love story. Keep on creatively writing it!

THE
BREAKUP

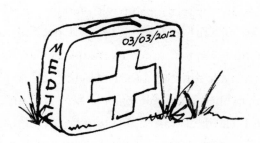

AUDREY

On March 3, 2012, I almost ruined our love story.

Our cross-country team wasn't meeting for practice that day, so I set out for my forty-five-minute easy run on my own. I headed into the wheat fields of Corvallis with Needtobreathe blaring through my headphones but turned it off about halfway through my run. I needed to finish my run in silence.

For several months, I had been feeling stressed, burned-out, and overwhelmed. I was desperate for direction from the Lord, especially about my relationship with Jeremy. In recent weeks, I had been wrestling with the feeling that I needed to break up with him. Having a long-distance relationship was challenging, and I felt like a horrible girlfriend for not being able to give my all to our relationship. When I commit to something, I'm an all-in kind of girl. The more I felt like I wasn't able to give my all to our relationship, the more I wanted to break it off before it failed.

As I ran back toward campus, I became increasingly sure I needed to break things off, but even the consideration of ending our love story pierced my heart. Conflicting thoughts swirled in my brain as I made my way back through campus, dodging all the bodies and backpacks. I felt like I was running in slow motion, but the illusion only made me want to run faster. Suddenly, I felt a very sharp pain in my stomach that made it difficult to breathe. I stopped running and hunched over to catch my breath. When

I tried to stand tall again, the pain grew worse. *This isn't right.* I called my roommate to pick me up and started to pass out while talking with her.

I had actually been battling stomach issues for about a year. It seemed like everything I ate made me sick. I often woke up with a really bad heartburn feeling that made breathing uncomfortable, and running always seemed to aggravate my stomach pain. I was determined to compete in the spring track season, so I continued to train through most of my pain and discomfort. But since it had been months, I started to seek medical advice.

That year, I spent more time in doctor appointments than I did in class. I saw gastroenterologists, naturopaths, nutritionists, allergists, and acupuncturists. I was diagnosed with irritable bowel syndrome, an amoeba, gallbladder issues, and food allergies, but none of the corresponding treatments gave me much relief. In addition to doctor appointments, I spent a significant amount of time cooking and grocery shopping, trying to find things I could make with ingredients that met my dietary restrictions, such as egg whites, meat, veggies, some fruits, nuts, and lots of coconut milk products. I was also actively involved as a volunteer leader in a high school ministry called Young Life. Oh yeah, and I was taking a hefty load of classes in school. It was all just too much. I was stressed-out, overwhelmed, and running myself into the ground.

Perhaps you know the verse, "I can do all things through Christ who strengthens me" (Philippians 4:13 NKJV). There are a lot of verses like that in the Bible. And they are the kind of verses that helped me to persevere through challenges for most of my high school and college life. However, my mom also often reminded me, "You can do all things, but not all at the same time."

In addition to verses about perseverance, there are also a lot of verses in the Bible about *rest*. "In quietness and trust is your strength," writes the prophet Isaiah (Isaiah 30:15). And Jesus himself says, "Come to me, all you who are weary and burdened, and I will give you rest" (Matthew 11:28). Up to this point, these were verses I had mostly ignored.

Ironically, or providentially, I was right in front of the student health building when I passed out. You can't make this stuff up! Apparently, someone had seen a distressed runner collapse in the middle of the road and called the paramedics. Within minutes, I heard sirens and felt the gawking eyes of curious college students standing nearby. I felt so embarrassed by this public display of weakness that I was determined to fight for consciousness just so I could refuse the paramedics' care. I was not about to be that girl.

Before the ambulance arrived, a doctor from the student health center came to my rescue, wheeled me into the health center, and hooked me up to some monitors. The paramedics from the ambulance, who had arrived in the meantime, followed me into the room to make sure I was okay. I don't remember much about what happened next, except that the student health doctor expressed concern about my heart rate and wanted to give me something to slow it down. Through exhausted breaths and blurry vision, I emphatically refused all medical intervention. Then I sat in one of the emergency care rooms until my pulse slowed and I was able to breathe normally.

The doctors wanted to run more tests, but I insisted on leaving. I didn't want to sit there talking to some student health doctor who thought she was going to solve my mysterious health problems on the spot. I had been to dozens of doctors and done countless tests, but no one had been able to give me any clear answers. I was fed up with trial and error. I blamed the incident on my chronic stomach issues, but in hindsight, I think I had an anxiety attack. All the physical, mental, and emotional stress had pushed me to the edge of a cliff, and contemplating ending things with Jeremy just pushed me over the edge. I knew what I needed most in that moment, and it wasn't drugs or tests. I didn't need medical intervention; I needed Jesus intervention. And I wasn't going to get that at the student health center.

I had planned to go to the beach that weekend with one of my college mentors, Shirley, and a few of my roommates. I had two women I considered my mentors throughout college. They were my therapists, my prayer warriors, my biggest fans, and my truth-sayers. I wouldn't have made it through college without Shirley and Jamie. Lord bless them, they kept me buoyant.

Every term, Shirley hosted a weekend silent retreat at the coast with a small group of women. We'd spend twenty-four hours in silence and then break our silence with a meal and a time of sharing what we sensed God had whispered to us in the quiet. I was determined to refuse medical care because I didn't want to miss the silent retreat I so desperately needed.

On the sixty-minute ride to the coast, everyone else in the car was chatting, but I started my silent retreat early. I spent the drive staring out the window and contemplating how to talk to Jeremy. I hated the thought of sending the dreaded "we need to talk" text. He knew I was going on silent retreat for the weekend, so he texted me to wish me a good time. I texted back that I would call him when we arrived so we could talk before I shut off my phone for the weekend.

When we arrived, everyone went inside to get settled, while I went out to the garage to call Jeremy. I ended up being there for three hours. I started off by apologizing for being such a horrible girlfriend and for not being able to give to our relationship what I desired to give to it. I hadn't been able to visit because I was training or competing year-round for cross-country and track on the weekends, and during the week I was in school or going to doctor appointments. Feeling like I was only on the receiving end of the relationship had started to wear on me.

I acknowledged how hard it was to hear all the stories of his adventures and the new friends he was making when my life was so stressful in comparison. It had become increasingly hard for me to relate and connect. I didn't know how to talk to him about my health problems and emotional burdens. I was so stressed from being sick that I began to wonder if stress was what was actually making me sick. If my illness continued, I was scared that Jeremy's emotional walls might prevent him from loving me through it. In an effort to prevent future heartache, I had to break up with him before it reached that point.

After telling him about collapsing on my run, I segued into the breakup talk. "With everything going on in my life right now, I just feel like I don't have anything left to give to our relationship," I said. "I need to focus on my health and school and running. I'm so emotionally drained."

His gracious response made it even more difficult for me to proceed. "Audrey, we don't have to talk every day," he said, "and you don't need to do anything for me. I don't want you to feel stressed. I want to be here for you."

"Yes, I know," I said, "but I just need to take a break." *Silence.* I could feel the weight of my words crushing him through the phone.

"I don't really believe in breaks," he finally said. "Are you sure you want to do this? I'm okay with letting our relationship take a back seat for a while, but do we really have to break up?"

"I just know I need to do this," I said. "I'm not saying anything is forever, but I need to release the emotional commitment of our relationship right now." I finally told him I had to go, and that I was turning off my phone for the next two days. I spent the rest of the weekend reading my Bible, praying, and crying.

O Lord, I feel a sense of release since breaking up, but am I just giving up? Should I have continued, knowing it would be hard? Lord, show Jeremy what you want to show him during this time. Don't let this hinder his walk with you, but rather show him what you want him to do. Make it clear to him if it will mean waiting for me or letting me go. Give him understanding about why I needed to do this and give him peace in the midst of confusion.

Jeremy called me on Sunday evening, but our conversation only went in circles—he trying to convince me I was making a mistake, and me trying to stand by the decision I felt so strongly was the only way forward. We eventually said good-bye and hung up. A few minutes later, Jer called me back, and I could tell he was holding back tears.

"Wait, so are we really broken up?" he asked. "I don't want to."

I was breaking my own heart and crushing Jeremy's.

Boating together early on in our friendship.

The bucket list we made at the beginning of the summer before we were dating.

A creative gift Jeremy made for Audrey when he was home for winter break.

Walking our trestle on the day we "pushed the envelope."

Hanging out while Jer was home to work pumpkin season—the day after Audrey finally said "I love you."

The photo we took on our first official date (not the blind date).

Audrey in Costa Rica with Jeremy's family.

Valentine's Day giant kiss that Audrey made and sent Jeremy during long distance.

Jeremy picking up running in Costa Rica, inspired by "the principle of sharing."

Jeremy reading *A Severe Mercy* aloud to Audrey in the airport.

The gingerbread house that won "most creative" during our trip to Black Butte.

Audrey playing in the annual Roloff Thanksgiving soccer game, inspired by "the principle of sharing."

Jeremy and Audrey with Mitch and Kelcey—the friends who
introduced them on the blind date.

Audrey's first time visiting Santa Barbara—exploring in Blue Moon.

Tye French

Moments after Jeremy proposed to Audrey under their beloved trestle.

Christianne Taylor

The first look on our wedding day.

Jeremy learns to ski, inspired by "the principle of sharing."

Late summer cruise in Bertha.

NeedToBreathe concert with friends while living in Bend.

Writing on our typewriter to announce that we're having a baby!

In our new house with Ember!

5

THE WAY
Forward

AUDREY

After the breakup, our love story entered a painful four-month hiatus during which I often Googled things like "best songs to get you through a heartbreak." We both felt it was probably best if we didn't communicate, although neither of us held to that completely. We were living separate lives and trying our best not to think about each other, but we still sent occasional "Don't forget about me" texts and secretly stalked each other on social media. You know, classic breakup stuff.

During our breakup, I continued to focus on my health, which began showing minor signs of improvement, and I was able to compete in the spring track season. I even put down a few good races, despite being emotionally and physically afflicted. After wrapping up the school year in June, I moved to Eugene for the first half of the summer, where I had a marketing internship with TrackTown USA for the 2012 US Olympic Trials.

It had been four months since we'd broken up when I got a text from Jeremy saying he was home on one of his two-week breaks and asking if we could meet up. Since we hadn't been talking much, I hadn't told him I'd accepted the internship. Although Eugene is only a couple of hours from our hometown, I also hadn't made any attempt to meet up with Jeremy while he was in Oregon. Cold, I know, but I just wasn't ready. I knew if we started to talk again, it would mean we were either done forever or were taking steps toward getting back together. And I wasn't ready for either.

Throughout the summer, I hung out with a few different guys, but they were all false starts. Jeremy was chased by a few different girls, but he never chased back. We both realized it was impossible to feel something with someone else after what we had. Our love was the realest thing either of us had ever experienced. Even though I still hadn't proclaimed "I love you" out loud, we were in love. And even though we were broken up, we hadn't fallen out of love. Everyone around us could see we were still committed to each other. I even told my roommates that I couldn't see myself marrying anyone else. When other girls expressed their feelings for Jeremy, his response was that he was still in love with me. We both had an underlying confidence that our love would somehow endure.

* * *

For my twenty-first birthday, I had a bunch of my friends over to my parents' house for Mexican food and margaritas. The gang included a few different guys who were interested in dating me at the time. It was sort of comical. Jeremy happened to be in town that weekend with his best friend, Tye, from Santa Barbara. They showed up just as we were about to leave my parents' house to go country line dancing for the rest of the night. From afar, I saw them come through the back gate. My whole body got really hot, and I felt completely flustered. *We haven't seen each other since breaking up and he decides to just show up at my birthday party unannounced?* I scanned the birthday party attendees, trying to decipher who might have invited him. Then I remembered I had casually told my mom that Jeremy was in town for a couple of weeks and that I was thinking about seeing him. But I didn't think she would go off on her own and invite him for my birthday!

"Hey, I didn't know you were coming," I said rudely as I gave him an awkward hug while looking over his shoulder to give my mom a reprimanding glare.

"Happy birthday, Auj," he replied kindly. "Yeah, I just thought I'd stop by while I was in town and say hi to your parents."

"Oh, cool," I said. "And good to see you, Tye! Well, we were just about to head out, but maybe we can connect later while you're here?"

"Yes, let's!" he said, grinning from ear to ear.

My goodness, he was cute. And he was wearing a pair of glasses that made him seem so much wiser and more mature than the last time I'd seen him. We texted later that night and agreed to meet up the next day. I had a hunch we would both profess our desire to be together again, which made me contemplate bailing, but I didn't.

We met at our spot—the trestle. I parked my car up the road and walked toward the bridge to climb into Bertha, Jer's 1969 GMC truck (yes, *another* vintage car). As I approached the bridge, I caught a glimpse of our shoes still proudly hanging from the wire.

A tsunami wave of memories rushed over me, and I regretted that I had so abruptly closed the book on the love story we were writing. We sat in the truck and began to unpack the past four months. We both wanted things to work out, but we knew things had to change for us to move forward.

I finally admitted my fear that he would not love me through my illness. I told him I felt like he wasn't getting what I was going through, and that made me feel even more distant from him. He apologized for his lack of encouragement and compassion and committed to being a better support. When he asked why I hadn't just told him up front what I needed, I told him I didn't want him to think of me as high-maintenance or a burden. If only I had been brave and honest enough to communicate my frustrations, I could have saved us both a boatload of heartbreak.

That conversation at the trestle was a critical juncture in our relationship. I finally trusted Jeremy with more of my heart. I learned to let him love me through my illness instead of using my illness as a pretext to push him away. As we lingered at the trestle, waiting for the train to pass by overhead, we caught each other up on the past four months. Jeremy prodded about the other guys who were at my birthday party, and I prodded about the girls I'd seen him with in Facebook photos. Our responses were the same—reassuring smiles. In a way, we had remained committed to each other. After all, that was largely what our long-distance relationship was anyway—friends who talked on the phone and who were committed to one day being together forever. After exchanging a few "I miss you"s and "I'm sorry"s but still no "I love you"s, we were back together. But this time it was different.

For the remainder of Jeremy's time at home, we spent nearly every day together. It was in those days that I started to realize how much I really did love Jeremy, although I still hadn't said "I love you." Ouch, I know. It was on the tip of my tongue before he headed back to Santa Barbara, but I made the excuse that it was too soon after the breakup.

A couple of weeks later, I woke up from a vivid dream. I'm not usually one for remembering my dreams or writing them down— that was more of a Jeremy thing—but this one felt significant. In the dream, I told Jeremy I loved him, and then everything about our relationship changed. When I woke up, there was no doubt in my mind that I loved him and that I needed to tell him. After scribbling down the dream in my journal, I headed off to morning practice. During my entire run, I kept thinking about what an idiot I was for not telling Jeremy I loved him when he was home. I didn't want to wait any longer, but I also didn't want to tell him on the phone—*how lame and anticlimactic.*

On my way home from morning practice, I got a call from Jeremy. The first thing he said when I answered the phone was, "Hey, Auj, did you have a dream last night?"

I didn't respond for a moment. Telling him about the conversation in the dream would have been royally awkward since I hadn't actually told him I loved him in real life. I tried to play it down. "I guess I did. Why?"

"Well, a bunch of friends and I had a time of fellowship last night. We were talking and worshiping and praying, and one of my friends prayed specifically for you to have a dream of clarity about our relationship. So I just thought I'd ask if ya did. Ha!" His tone indicated that he didn't actually think the prayer would be answered.

"Oh wow, crazy," I said. "I can't really remember my dream though . . . Hey, I gotta go. I'll call you later." I was stunned. I had to get off the phone before I started to sound suspicious.

Later that day, I went on a walk with my friend and mentor Jamie Herb—not Shirley, she's the silent retreat one. Jamie's husband, Chris, was the Young Life area director for my college town. When I started leading and attending the college Young Life Bible study, I met Jamie, and we hit it off. Soon after meeting her, we began getting together every other week. Jamie walked with me through my dating relationship, my sickness, the breakup, the getting back together, and all the highs and lows in between.

While we were strolling along the river, I told her about the dream and Jeremy's call. She gasped and then laughed in amazement, agreeing it was definitely time I said the L-word. I came to terms with the fact that I would have to tell Jeremy on the phone or by Skype; otherwise, I'd have to wait another couple of months before I saw him again, and I knew I couldn't wait that long. I was finally ready, and all of a sudden it seemed urgent. Then I caught a break when I talked to Jeremy later that day and he told me he would be coming home in a couple of weeks for the first weekend of pumpkin season. *Praise hands!*

The weekend he came back, we made plans to have dinner together, and I promised myself I would tell him by the end of the night. I was so nervous/excited that I thought the butterflies in my stomach just might carry me to the sky. Wow, this moment was two and a half years in the making! I hardly touched my dinner, which was so unlike me.

When we got in the truck to drive back to the farm, Jer took the long way home. As we wound our way through the hills of Northwest Portland I was quiet. Jer tried to engage in conversation, asking questions and making comments about how happy he was that we were together again. Poor guy must have thought I was about to break up with him again, based on how withdrawn I was from the conversation. I was so focused on convincing myself not to chicken out and on contemplating how I would say it—my long-awaited confession of love.

We pulled up to the farmhouse, and right as Jer was about to turn off the engine, I reached over and placed my hand on his right arm. He looked at me, dropped his arm away from the key, and reached over to put his hand on my leg. The bench in the truck allowed us to sit side by side with nothing between us. "Jeremy . . . I love you." *Phew! I did it.*

Jer's jaw literally dropped. He kissed me and then pulled away to look me in the eyes. I'd never seen him smile so big. "Say it again!"

I laughed and obliged. "I love you, babe."

He lifted his hand from my leg and gently placed it on the side of my face, running his thumb slowly across my cheekbone. "I love you *too*." He said that fourth word made all the difference.

When I got in my car to drive home, I felt like a whole new person. I realized that saying I love you was the only way forward. Just as it was in my dream, it changed everything for us. The verbal proclamation gave way to a heart transformation.

In some ways, it reminded me of how I felt after verbally committing my life to the Lord in baptism. I knew and loved Jesus before I was baptized, but everything changed after making a public confession of my faith and getting dunked. I went from wanting to know more about Jesus to talking about him incessantly—from irregular interest to faithful pursuit.

Confessing my love to Jeremy was a similar experience—I went "public" with my heart. All of a sudden, I became a lot more giddy and girly too. It was like all those years of bottled-up emotion were oozing out of me, and there was no putting a lid on it.

JEREMY

My childhood and adolescence weren't what most people would consider typical. Both my parents are dwarfs, and my twin brother Zach is also a dwarf. My two younger siblings, Molly and Jacob, are average height like me. Our family situation was unique enough that it wasn't long before we started to catch some attention from the media. After dozens of newspaper interviews and talk show appearances, TLC network executives approached our family with an offer to do a reality television show. I was fourteen years old at the time, and reality television was still in its infancy.

My parents agreed to give it a whirl, and in the fall of 2005, we started filming a show called *Little People, Big World*. At the time of this writing, the show is heading into its thirteenth season. We now hold the Guinness World Record for "the most episodes of a family-focused television show." With fame came both opportunity and obstacles. However, those are stories for another book. What I will say is that both the farm and the show have intricately shaped the way I think, act, and love.

I believe much of my passion for life came from the freedom I had to build, create, and explore whatever I wanted on the farm. I was always a passionate kid, often described by my teachers as "a romantic" or "an old soul." I even won character awards for persuasion and passion. I channeled my passion into exploring the land, building forts, restoring old cars, and creating inventions.

But I need to make a quick distinction here. I was passionate, but never emotional. In fact, it was pursuing my passions that actually allowed me to hide my emotions—from others and sometimes even from myself. There was always something to do at the farm, which kept me busy and distracted, especially from dealing with anything difficult or sad. I always had a car in the barn, a fort in the woods, or something that needed tending to that provided an escape when things got emotional.

The farm also gave me a strong sense of story. All of the creations my dad had built and the projects I found myself working on were brimming with story. The cowboy town told stories of the Old West and settling the American frontier. The pirate ship and castle brought to life the movie *Hook* and tales of white knights. When the images you read about are brought to life in front of your very own eyes, it's impossible not to get wrapped up in the stories.

The farm gave me a worldview of life as a grand adventure—a big story—and I wanted to live into it. This idea has faithfully showed up throughout my life by helping me zoom out and look at the big picture. All stories have a beginning, a middle, and an end. Looking at my life as a grand narrative has helped me make decisions based on the overall story. For example, when I began dating Audrey, I instinctively imagined what the result of my actions would be in light of the overall story I was in. A question I often ask myself when making decisions is, "Is this the story I want to tell?"

Little People, Big World also shaped me in profound ways. There were obvious benefits, such as the ability to travel the world and do things I never thought I'd be able to do. But when you grow up on TV, life comes at you harder and faster than normal. People take a greater interest in what you say, wear, and do than they otherwise would. It wasn't until I saw the ugly side of fame that I understood how careful I needed to be when I was in the public eye. Innocent intentions don't necessarily matter when millions of people from all kinds of backgrounds are watching you and drawing their own conclusions about everything you say and do. After navigating the chaos of rumors in the media, I realized that the less I revealed, the less people would know and the less I would be judged. These were my walls of self-protection.

Over time, I became somewhat of a paradox—both a passionate romantic and an emotional recluse. Outwardly, I appeared to be the same Jer—loud, funny, often the center of attention—but inwardly, I was on lockdown. As the years of filming continued, I built up more and more emotional barricades to protect myself. Without realizing it, I was living by the principle, *If I don't give people bullets, they can't shoot me.* I held my cards close, and my emotions closer. It served me well in my younger years. It kept me closed off, safe, and wary. It protected me from getting caught up with the wrong kind of girls and illegitimate friendships. But the emotional stronghold that kept me safe as a kid eventually became an emotional prison that kept me distant from the girl I had fallen in love with.

When Audrey came into the picture, the focus of my passion suddenly shifted. I no longer channeled all of my energy into all of my interests in and around the farm. I had found what would become the best focus for expressing my love—Audrey. But it wasn't just expression that Audrey was after; it was my heart. I didn't realize how formidable my emotional walls had become until Audrey called me out on it.

It happened late one night after everyone went to bed. Auj and I were staying with her family at their vacation home in Bend, Oregon, and we stayed up a little later by the fire. Audrey addressed the emotional walls she saw in me, and to my displeasure, she began to identify them. She pointed out that I never wanted to talk about "how I feel" about certain things, and how I masterfully navigated out of conversations that were emotional or personal.

Audrey was starting to draw parallels on her own. She'd ask penetrating questions like, "Did always having to talk about your relationships with your family members on TV affect the depth of your relationships with them? How do you handle all the nasty comments and messages from people on social media? Do you feel like you've had to defend yourself your whole life? Do the TV producers project an image on you that you feel like you have to live up to?"

I remember thinking, *How does she even know to ask this stuff?* We had a long and difficult conversation because—proving her point—it was something I didn't want to talk about . . . but knew I needed to. There's only one thing I hate more than talking about my emotions—going to the dentist. And this conversation felt a lot like lying back in the dreaded chair under the lights and letting the dental hygienist clean and floss my teeth. I know it's good for me, but it's uncomfortable, painful, and invasive. Here was Audrey trying to floss my heart, and just like flossing, if you don't do it on a regular basis, it hurts a little more when you do.

Audrey asked me some deeply personal and never-before-talked-about stuff—a task reserved for the most trusted allies, and that's what we had become. Our friendship did what all healthy friendships tend to do—it sharpened us and made us better versions of ourselves. It shared truth with love. Among other things, Audrey helped me see that I lacked compassion and empathy, and that I often caged up my emotions instead of expressing them. She pointed out that perhaps the TV show had numbed my emotional response to the hard stuff life threw my way. I had never really thought about any of the things she was bringing up.

Audrey pointed out some ways I could improve that I might have otherwise just accepted as part of my personality and ignored. True love has a way of calling us out of our dark hiding places and into the light of freedom. And I did feel more free after our conversation. Although I didn't share everything with Auj that night, I shared more with her than I had with anyone before, and she prevented the hidden spots in my heart from harboring decay. This conversation with Auj was cavity prevention, and although it was one of the first such talks, it definitely wasn't the last.

AUDREY

To this day, Jeremy and I are on a never-ending pursuit of being fully known and fully loved. Since being married, we discovered a brilliant tool called the Enneagram (pronounced *enny-a-gram*) that has helped us as we seek to understand each other more and love each other better. This personality typing system helps people better understand themselves and the people in their lives. It outlines nine personality types, each with its own distinct strategies for relating to self, others, and the world. Each type also has its own pattern of thinking, feeling, and acting that arises from its distinctive motivation and worldview.

I wish we would have known about the Enneagram when we were dating. It has helped me understand why I was so reluctant to share about my sickness with Jeremy and ask him for help. It has helped me understand why it took me forever to say "I love you" back. It has helped Jeremy understand why he never wanted to talk about his emotions. Learning our Enneagram numbers has given us a much deeper understanding of ourselves and each other, which has enabled us to love each other better.

The nine Enneagram types are identified by number. I am an Eight, which is sometimes called "the Challenger." The key motivations of Eights are to be self-reliant, to prove their strength and resist weakness, and to be important in their world. *Me in a nutshell.* No wonder I acted like I didn't care about my boyfriends and took forever to say "I love you." Eights are self-confident, strong, assertive, protective, and decisive, but they can also be egocentric and domineering. *Unfortunately, also me.* Eights feel they must control their environment, especially people, sometimes becoming confrontational and intimidating. *Bashful hand raise.* Eights typically have problems allowing themselves to be vulnerable—hence my stubborn walls. *Yeah.*

Each Enneagram type has what's called a "basic fear." For the Eight, it is the fear of being harmed or controlled by others. Here's how the Enneagram Institute describes it:

> Beneath their imposing exterior, Eights often feel hurt and rejected, although this is something they seldom talk about because they have trouble admitting their vulnerability to themselves, let alone to anyone else. Because they fear that they will be rejected . . . Eights attempt to defend themselves by rejecting others first. The result is that average Eights become *blocked in their ability to connect with people* or to love since love gives the other power over them, reawakening their Basic Fear.[1]

I laughed the first time I read this because it felt as though a spotlight was shining a white-hot light on my soul. All of this helps explain why I initially resisted Jeremy's pursuit and kept my heart guarded for so long.

Jeremy is an Enneagram Nine. The Nine is often called "the Peacemaker" because they are devoted to internal and external peace for themselves and others. They can be described as easygoing, trusting, patient, distracted, and indecisive. Healthy Nines are often indomitable, which may be why Jeremy was so determined to figure me out and get past my walls.

According to the Enneagram Institute, Nines are often referred to as "*the crown of the Enneagram* because it is at the top of the symbol and because it seems to include the whole of it. Nines can have the strength of Eights, the sense of fun and adventure of Sevens, the dutifulness of Sixes, the intellectualism of Fives, the creativity of Fours, the attractiveness of Threes, the generosity of Twos, and the idealism of Ones."[2] Yes, I married up!

Nines can also be described as dreamers, and I think this contributes to why Jeremy felt so alive growing up on the farm— building forts, driving tractors, fixing up old cars, and dreaming up new adventures. I think his dreamer mentality is also what kept him believing in a love story worth reading one day.

But as I've said before, Jeremy is not perfect. Nines have weaknesses too. They generally don't have a strong sense of their own identity. Nines may think they're maintaining the peace, but, really, they're just "numbing out." I think growing up in the public eye enhanced this for Jeremy.

Nines also respond to difficult situations, pain, and suffering with a premature peace. I think this is part of the reason I felt that Jeremy didn't, or wouldn't be able to, understand the difficulty of my illness. Sure, some of that was because of my walls, but in hindsight, Jeremy had some walls too. I discovered his wall of emotional detachment when I confronted him in Bend about how the show had impacted his life and how he felt about the baggage that came with growing up in the public eye. His response was optimistic, reserved, and unemotional. It wasn't until the days leading up to our wedding that Jeremy's emotional walls were finally breached.

Here's what the Enneagram Institute has to say about Eights and Nines in relationship:

Nines bring a sense of calm and stability that Eights find soothing and necessary for their wellbeing. They also bring to Eights a feeling of quiet pride in the Eight's bravado and more assertive qualities, encouraging Eights to continue in their take charge style. Even healthy Eights spend a lot of time overcoming obstacles and adversity; they are fighters trying to survive and make their mark on the world. Nines are like a safe harbor, a respite, a person with whom Eights can let down their guard and relax. They tend therefore to teach each other what the other lacks: Eights bring Nines self-confidence and self-assertion, while Nines teach Eights which battles are worth fighting for and how not to push so hard. The Eight/ Nine couple is thus like fire and water—an active force and a receptive force—that has an archetypal feeling about it . . . Both have powerful drives and strong willpower; both like comfort and simplicity; both want to create a safe retreat from the world. When these forces and their talents are harnessed together after the same goals, this pair can be dynamic and powerful but also comfortable and receptive at the same time.[3]

Totally us. I wish we had known about this sooner in our relationship! Discovering our types has enabled us to love, connect, reconcile, and understand each other in a whole new way. Part of self-reflection is self-awareness. We can't change something we aren't aware of. The Enneagram helped us understand each other in more profound and meaningful ways, which helped us communicate our thoughts, desires, and frustrations with greater clarity and ease.

Whether you're single, dating, or married, find out your Enneagram number. For us, it has been a transformative tool—a way forward—as we continue to learn how to love each other better. The best way to figure out your Enneagram number is to read about each number on the Enneagram Institute's website (www.enneagraminstitute.com), or you can take the Riso-Hudson Enneagram Type Indicator (RHETI—the most accurate test) to help you determine your dominant type. The Enneagram Institue unpacks each number in depth and gives insight into your compatibility with other Enneagram types. As Jer and I read our descriptions, we were shocked at how perfectly they illustrated our innermost thoughts, motivations, fears, and desires.

*   *   *

I'll be honest, along with being an Enneagram Eight, I think I was influenced by all the hard-to-get girls in the chick flicks. You know, Allie in *The Notebook*, Melanie in *Sweet Home Alabama*, or Jamie in *A Walk to Remember*. They acted like they didn't care, even though they really did. They had walls. They were stubborn. They stuffed their insecurities and buried their struggles and fears. They masqueraded themselves as hard to get, but deep down they were madly in love. Maybe the entertainment industry brainwashed me into being that girl and fed me the lie that in order to be loved, I had to be hard to get. In other words, *If he really knew me, maybe he wouldn't love me.*

I love how author and pastor Timothy Keller describes it in his book *The Meaning of Marriage*: "To be loved but not known is comforting but superficial. To be known and not loved is our greatest fear. But to be fully known and truly loved is, well, a lot like being loved by God. It is what we need more than anything. It liberates us from pretense, humbles us out of our self-righteousness, and fortifies us for any difficulty life can throw at us."[4]

We can fake love or fear not being loved, but both of these options eventually leave us heartbroken. To be fully known and fully loved—that's where the wholeness of love is experienced. And that's how holiness in love is expressed: "There is no fear in love. But perfect love drives out fear" (1 John 4:18). Jer and I both wanted to be *fully known and truly loved*, but fear, pride, and misunderstanding held us back.

Every relationship experiences a critical juncture, or perhaps a few of them. Critical junctures are defining moments in the relationship when you and your partner decide to break up or get serious, to give up or determine to find *the way forward*. Our way forward was a vulnerable and honest conversation under the trestle before getting back together. It was me finally saying "I love you" to Jeremy for the first time. It was Jeremy finally embracing his emotional side and opening up about things he had never talked about with anyone before. It was then that we understood each other's emotional core and experienced what it was like to be fully known and fully loved.

6

THE
Principle of Sharing

JEREMY

The longest we went without seeing each other was three months. My family had decided to go to Costa Rica on vacation, and I would be missing two weeks of school in order to join them. That meant I had to forgo several of my routine visits back home in order to complete all of my schoolwork before the trip. The good news—Audrey would be joining us! The bad news—after a three-month separation, our reunion would take place in an airport lounge and be filmed by the camera crew from *Little People, Big World* for later broadcast. *Yikes!*

Audrey flew with my family from Portland to Dallas, and I met them at the Dallas airport en route to Costa Rica. The cameras rolled as I entered the airport lounge and embraced Audrey. Our long-awaited reunion was a bit embarrassing, probably more so for

Audrey, but we were together again, and that was all that mattered. While waiting for our connection, I pulled a book out of my bag and suggested to Auj that we read it together.

The book was *A Severe Mercy* by Sheldon Vanauken, and it tells the story of his relationship with his wife, Davy. I read the book a year earlier, and it profoundly influenced me—so much so that I committed to reading it once every year. I have since read it seven times and just began my eighth. The book has become a well of inspiration I continue to draw from, and I feel a soul connection to the grand story that Sheldon tells.

Audrey liked the idea of reading together, so we snuck away from the rest of the family and the film crew and found a quiet gate area where we began reading aloud. From the first sentence I read, Audrey's face lit up. I could tell she would feel a soul connection to the story too. We continued to read it together throughout the trip. More about that to come.

Costa Rica was the first trip we went on together, and it satisfied our longing to share experiences together rather than having to relay our separate experiences over the phone. For once, I didn't have to mail fragrant flowers, send a photo of my favorite beach, or read a line from my favorite book over the phone. We were together—smelling, seeing, and reading the same things—and we didn't take it for granted. We clung to the moments, squeezing hands a little tighter, holding our hugs a little longer, and enjoying just being in each other's presence.

One night, we took cover from a warm tropical rain and watched a storm roll in over the ocean. I hugged Auj as we looked out at the dark tumbling clouds playing with the sea, and then I looked at her and said, "Lock it in." She smiled, knowing exactly what I meant. This became the phrase we'd say to each other whenever we experienced moments we wanted to engrave in our memories. Giving voice to our desire to commemorate a moment enhanced our memory of it. We said it often throughout the trip, especially as we read *A Severe Mercy* on the beach or woke up early to read it by the pool before breakfast. We still say it from time to time when a moment calls for it.

While reading, we continually stopped to talk about the overall beauty of the Vanaukens' love story. Something about it heightened our awareness and our appreciation of the tropical beauty that surrounded us. We also took an interest in the principles the author described. Specifically, the principle of spontaneity, the principle of the affirmative, the principle of courtesy, and the principle of sharing. The principle that stuck out most to us was the principle of sharing.

* * *

Sheldon and his wife, Davy, were two lovers determined to reach the heights of love. After a small tiff, they found themselves in a discussion about how to make love endure. "What is it that draws two people into closeness and love?" they asked. And their answer: "Of course there's the mystery of physical attraction, but beyond that it's the things they share . . . Total sharing, we felt, was the ultimate secret of a love that would last for ever."[1]

People are bound together by what they share. Audrey and I share an affinity for old barns, campfires, antiques, and country things. More importantly, we share the same value system, the desire to raise a family, and a commitment to the Word of God. We also enjoy *talking* about all of these things we share. These commonalities between Audrey and me drew us together, but as our relationship progressed, we began to seek out more things to share and more ways to be intentional in becoming one.

Sheldon and Davy believed that if two people chose to share everything, they would continue to become closer and closer. Hence, the *principle of sharing*:

> If one of us likes *anything*, there must be something to like in it—and the other one must find it . . . That way we shall create a thousand strands, great and small, that will link us together. Then we shall be so close that it would be impossible—unthinkable—for either of us to suppose that we could ever recreate such closeness with anyone else. And our trust in each other will not only be based on love and loyalty but on the *fact* of a thousand sharings—a thousand strands twisted into something unbreakable.[2]

Through sharing, Sheldon and Davy fortified their bond of friendship and kept their feelings of in-loveness alive. With every passing year, they experienced a new depth of closeness, building an unbreakable strand of sharing that would weather any storm.

Even though we hadn't known about the principle, we recognized the truth of it in the development of our relationship. It was the principle of sharing that made a lasting memory of the half marathon I had run for Audrey. Although the race itself was miserable, it was something we shared (even though we didn't end up running it side by side). While in Costa Rica, I committed to take up running because it was something Audrey loved. After we were married, we eventually ran another half marathon, but this time we did it together, and I finished ten minutes behind her. To this day, we still go on runs together—it's become something I now enjoy, and it's a strand of sharing that draws us closer together.

Audrey and her family and friends are big gamers. When we first met, I played games only because Audrey was playing, but now I want to play them because I enjoy them too. Because games are something Audrey loves, I learned to love them too. In fact, we started playing chess together so much that Audrey even had a custom chess table made for me as a Christmas gift. Now we have a cabinet full of games, most of which I've bought—something I never thought I'd do!

We pressed into the principle of sharing, intent on discovering the good in whatever the other loved. Sharing builds closeness. Sheldon and Davy went so far as to read all of the same books in an attempt to know and understand each other completely.

Audrey and I took the principle of sharing one step further in a different way—by abstaining from the same things. For example, Audrey used to watch *The Bachelor*, and this was something I was not willing to share. I refused to watch it and didn't like the fact that she watched it. I have nothing against the people on the show; rather, I have something against how the shows represent true love and how we should go about looking for it.

Initially, Audrey's pushback was that watching these shows was something social to do with friends. She liked dissecting all of the different relationship issues that arose on the show. However, after a few months of low-key discussions about it and explaining to Audrey where I was coming from, she admitted that the show did violate the values and convictions we both have about love. Now she doesn't have any desire to watch it either. *The Bachelor/ Bachelorette* does not align with our collective values and therefore would have been a point of division.

Audrey gave it up in an effort to pursue our oneness and adhere to the principle of sharing. In this instance, the principle of sharing was about what we abstained from together rather than what we partook in together. During our first year of marriage, there was a period of time when in order to support and love Audrey, I shared with her by abstaining from gluten. By abstaining, I was able to briefly catch a glimpse of what she had to do for all her stomach issues. She felt supported and understood.

Of course, this will look different for everyone. We don't literally share absolutely everything. And yes, I have my own toothbrush. This is simply a principle to live by, and it can be applied however you please. While we were dating, we found it useful in learning about each other and our compatibility. While married, this principle has reminded us to keep on pursuing oneness as we make new friends, build a home, and begin to build a family.

AUDREY

There's nothing quite like reuniting with your boyfriend you haven't seen in three months in front of a camera crew. Among other things, I was afraid the audio guy would be able to hear how fast my heart was beating through the microphone I was wearing. I also remember thinking, *If I have to go to the bathroom, will he be listening to me pee?* Jer's family only added pressure to the situation with their wide-eyed, "Sooo . . . are you excited to see him?" interrogations. All of the other passengers in the airport lounge area were trying to discreetly capture photos of the spectacle that we were. When Jeremy walked into the room, I was shaking with nervous excitement. I could hardly muster the strength and coordination to stand up and hug him. In that moment, I wished no one was there, but it felt like everyone was there.

We hugged, and then his smile silenced my insecurities. He handed me an envelope, which I waited to read until we were off camera. I could tell he was a little flustered to see me too, which was comforting in a way. For the past few weeks, I had been waffling about whether to go on the trip. I was eager for an opportunity to be with Jeremy, but my health concerns had me worried about traveling internationally.

Three months prior to the trip, my stomach issues had become so serious that I was forced to take a term off from school and put my running career on hold. I spent my days doing one of three things: visiting doctors, preparing meals, or agonizing in bed. I was deeply discouraged and desperate for healing. It was a horribly dark time in my life but also a time in which the Lord reminded me that just being with him was enough. Instead of trying to control everything, I learned how to make surrender and trust a daily practice. That turned out to be vital training that would help me endure trials in the years to come. And perhaps most importantly, I learned to ask for help.

During the time I was sick, Jeremy was so understanding and patient with my gloomy, Eeyore-like responses. He continued to listen to me, encourage me, and love me through this very hard time when I did not feel like myself at all. When he invited me to go to Costa Rica with his family for spring break, I initially declined. I just assumed all of my dietary restrictions meant traveling to a Third World country was out of the question. However, I had finally started to show some signs of improvement, and when I talked to my parents, friends, and doctors about the possibility of going, I was surprised that they all encouraged me to go. I think everyone felt so bad about my physical health that they saw it as a good prescription for my emotional and mental healing. Sunshine, waves, and love can heal anything, right?

During the trip, I had a long list of dietary restrictions, and I had to be meticulous about drinking solely bottled water, using it even to brush my teeth. All my health restrictions required me to be very communicative with Jer about what I needed and how I felt. It also gave him an opportunity to feel needed and useful, which was a good thing, even though it made me feel high-maintenance. Asking for help and allowing Jeremy to take care of me were things I needed to learn how to do.

Costa Rica was another milestone marker in our relationship. It was our first trip together; my first time appearing on *Little People, Big World*; my first time spending extended time with Jer's family; Jer's first time having to take care of me; our first time reading *A Severe Mercy* together; and the beginning of our commitment to the principle of sharing. Even though back home we were still separated by distance, we wanted to be joined by emotional togetherness.

While we were in Costa Rica, I realized that one of the gaps that separated us was soccer. The World Cup was happening, and Jer's family convened in the hotel lobby in the evenings to watch the games. I had never played soccer and definitely didn't have a desire to watch it. But it was clear that Jeremy's entire family took the game seriously and that Jeremy loved it. So I attempted to show interest. As I was learning through reading *A Severe Mercy*, if Jeremy loved soccer, there must be something about it to love.

I watched him play in indoor games when he came home to visit in the summer. I learned to kick a soccer ball on the beach when I visited him in Santa Barbara. For his birthday, I gave him a soccer backpack from his favorite team. I even played in the Roloff family's annual Thanksgiving Day soccer game one year. By sharing in all of these things and learning to love soccer, I came to understand why Jeremy loved soccer, which helped me to better love and understand him.

Jeremy always referred to soccer as "the world's language," and when we were in Costa Rica, I saw just how true that is. Over breakfast or while out on an excursion, Jeremy would often make a comment to one of the locals about the World Cup. Within seconds, he seemed to have a new best friend. Everyone we met in Costa Rica loved soccer. Talking about it was a way for Jeremy to connect with people. As I watched him, I came to understand Jeremy in new ways. This was one of the beautiful things about the principle of sharing. It allowed us to know each other better, which enabled us to love each other more.

Another thing I learned to love through the principle of sharing was old cars. We've talked about some of the fun adventures we had in Jeremy's vintage cars, but not the less-than-fun ones, like the times when his cars broke down or wouldn't start. This was, and still is, a regular occurrence. Yes, even now he still owns them all, but the inconvenience has never made me push him to sell. Call me crazy, but I've actually grown to love their imperfections and the stories that result from the times we've been suddenly stranded.

Throughout our dating relationship, Jeremy had four old cars. One was given to him; the others he bought on Craigslist and fixed up. There was the 1971 BMW 2002 (OhSo), the 1971 Volkswagen van (Blue Moon), the 1969 GMC truck (Bertha), and the 1976 Toyota FJ40 (Rain). Each car seemed to mark a different season of our relationship:

- OhSo = friend zone
- Blue Moon = falling in love and starting to date
- Bertha = the breakup
- Rain = the big question and the big day (more about that to come)

When we were together in Oregon, it would have been more convenient to take my car out to dinner, but I enjoyed moseying along the highway at 50 miles an hour in one of Jer's vintage treasures. I got a kick out of watching all of the husbands abruptly tap their wives and eagerly point to Jer's car with admiration and longing looks. I loved the ease of parking tiny OhSo, having space to hang out in the back of Blue Moon, cranking the manual windows in Bertha, and enjoying the quiet afforded by the lack of a stereo in Rain. We always exchanged smiles of relief when the cars started up on the first try, but even push-starting Blue Moon or conversing with the strangers who offered to give us a jump was fun.

So many of our richest conversations took place in these old vehicles, which is part of the reason I don't mind still having them around. The nostalgia is too precious. And they continue to solicit adventure while inviting us to practice extending grace toward one another—for example, a couple of years ago when I found myself waving the jumper cables in the snow after we broke down in Rain while getting our Christmas tree. Or—you moms will get a kick out of this one—when we broke down in the Costco parking lot while I was eight months pregnant and it was 90 degrees out. Yes, we are still married, and yes, we still own Rain.

Although I just gave you two examples of sticky situations that I handled with patience and grace, let me be really clear—Jeremy and I are *not* perfect. We fight. We let our emotions get the best of us sometimes. We blame each other instead of the circumstances. We forget that we are on the same team. But the more we pursue the principle of sharing, the more we enable moments bound for strife to be met with grace-giving smiles.

JEREMY

Auj and I are continuing to learn that if one of us loves something that falls in line with our shared values, then there must be something in it to love. And when the other is willing to find whatever there is in it to love, we get to experience a greater closeness and unity. Finding new things to love about each other is a gift that keeps on giving. It keeps alive the growing excitement of discovery as we not only unearth more to love about each other but fall deeper in love in the process. We believe that bridging the gap of separateness with strands of unity will continue to draw us closer together and that weeding out things that separate us will deepen our love.

Pre-marriage, we tried to close the gaps by sharing in our hobbies and interests. After marriage, we continue to do this in other areas as well—our failures, victories, responsibilities, and even the words we use. For example, in our house, it's my job to take out the trash. However, when I sometimes forget, Audrey gets frustrated and points out my fault. Likewise, I get frustrated with Audrey when we're running late because she's taking too long to get ready. I blame our tardiness on her.

We've been working on shifting the way we talk about these types of situations by using "we" instead of "you." We call it "we shifting." So instead of saying, "Jer, you forgot to take out the trash," Audrey says, "Jer, we forgot to take out the trash." And instead of saying, "Auj was running late," I say, "We are running late." It may seem like a small thing, but this simple change shifts the atmosphere and our attitudes from accusation to alliance and from separateness to togetherness. If we are indeed "one flesh," as Scripture proclaims we are, then we want to live into that in every way we can. We become one when we say "I do," but we also continue to become one through daily actions and words that proclaim "we do."

Sheldon and Davy Vanauken had a theory that "the killer of love is creeping separateness."[3] If sharing builds a thousand strands of unity that bind us together, it only makes sense that a thousand strands of separateness builds distance. It came as a bit of a shock that if we could sow closeness, we could also sow distance! Audrey and I had been forced to experience what physical distance does to love. Living individual lives, we entered a season of separateness during long distance that turned our flame of love into a smolder. Distance surely is the enemy of love!

We live in a world where genuine love—love that lasts—is hard to find. Love can be alive one moment and gone the next. We see this in the divorce rate, in broken families, in unfaithful spouses—fill in the blank. Love can flee as impulsively as the feelings do. We are a culture that chases feelings as the fruit of love, while neglecting to water the tree that produces the fruit. If feelings of love endured on their own accord, we would be seeing different results. However, it is apparent that the feelings of love don't last without the actions of love—watering the tree.

We believe that the principle of sharing is one good way to water the tree. I love how author Timothy Keller puts it, "Our culture says that feelings of love are the basis for actions of love. And of course that can be true. But it is truer to say that actions of love can lead consistently to feelings of love."[4]

Sheldon and Davy Vanauken discovered what they believed to be the guardian of true love—continual sharing. A lifetime devotion to ongoing discovery and pursuit of one another. Through continual sharing, they would build a wall of protection around their love.

I don't know about you, but I just love that. What a brilliant picture of two people desiring to get the most out of their love story. Sheldon and Davy's method might not be for you, but there is definitely truth in its application. Sharing will lead you toward closeness; separateness will move you away from it. If you're lobbying for separate lives, you will eventually have them. The principle of sharing is a mind-set that will save you time in the dating world as you look for a suitable spouse and continue to be a gift that keeps on giving in marriage.

7

LOSING THE
Purity Battle

AUDREY

We were virgins on our wedding night. But before you make us out to be unrelatable saints and skip this chapter, let me be real clear about something. Even though we won the virginity battle, we lost the purity battle. Sure, we saved the actual act of intercourse for marriage—and we're so thankful we did—but that's not even half the battle.

I'm going to go out on a limb here and say I don't think Jer and I are the only Christian couple who "waited" but also messed around. Maybe I just described the dating relationship you're in right now. Maybe you've found yourself hanging out in your boyfriend's bedroom late at night with candles lit and a glass of wine—tempted. Maybe you've found yourself cuddling on the couch when no one else was home, "watching a chick flick"—or should I say "making out"? Or maybe you found yourself in tears the next morning, ashamed of your inability to keep your clothes on last night. Yes, I just said that. And yes, Jer and I found ourselves in each of these situations. There is a reason the Bible says, "If they cannot control themselves, they should marry, for it is better to marry than to burn with passion" (1 Corinthians 7:9).

In the months leading up to our wedding day, we definitely *burned with passion.* To this day, Jeremy and I ache for our friends who choose to have long engagements, mostly for this reason. And yet many couples who are ready to get married put off their weddings for reasons that have little to do with their relationship and a lot to do with pressures and expectations driven by the media and the wedding industry. Everything must be "dream come true" perfect, right? So when the venue isn't available for another year and the dress won't come in for at least six months, the marriage is delayed for the sake of the wedding. Don't get me wrong, I loved planning an epic celebration, but I also think our culture has *overvalued* the day and *undervalued* the promise. In the same way, I think Christians especially have overvalued virginity and undervalued purity.

In the Bible, purity means to be morally clean and without blemish. Pursuing purity essentially means to pursue holiness with our minds, hearts, and bodies. To be pure means to be guiltless, blameless, and innocent. To believe that God's ways are the best ways and to walk in them. And when we walk in purity, we are wholly available to God, ready to be used to accomplish his purposes.

If your sexual past has left you feeling dirty, guilty, or impure, please hear this. God desires to wash you white as snow (Isaiah 1:18), to give you an undivided heart (Ezekiel 11:19), to renew a right spirit within you (Psalm 51:10). He delights to make you blameless and pure, without fault or blemish (Philippians 2:15) and free from guilt and shame.

Jeremy and I were both raised in Christian homes. Our parents and the church engraved in our minds that sex before marriage was bad. If you were a guy, you were taught to respect women and keep your hands to yourself. If you were a girl, you were taught to save yourself for your husband, and perhaps you were given a purity ring. Beyond that, we didn't get much practical guidance. When it came to such issues as pornography, dirty dancing, and the rest of the "bases," we were left to fend for ourselves.

I was the oldest child of three and raised in a pretty sheltered home. For example, I didn't see a movie with a sex scene in it until I was a freshman in high school. I remember being so embarrassed that I was the only one of my friends who still hadn't seen *The Titanic* in middle school because I wasn't allowed to watch R-rated movies. While the rest of my friends were buying push-up bras, wearing makeup, shaving their legs, and figuring out how to use tampons, I was still flat as a board, with a smile full of metal and no idea that getting to first base could refer to anything other than baseball.

Needless to say, the oversexed reality of high school was a bit of a shock. I attended one of the biggest public high schools in Portland, Oregon, which is where I learned to "grind" (to you older folks reading this, that is code for dirty dancing) and was dared to make out with a boy on my cross-country team on the bus ride home from a race. Taking the dare was my first kissing experience. Yikes! My point is that I was thrown into a world of lies about sex, purity, my body, and love. And that was nearly a decade ago, back in the days when Myspace had barely hit the scene and everyone still had flip phones that required you to delete your old text messages to make room for incoming texts. Remember that? Nowadays, middle schoolers have access to sex in the palm of their hands—and I don't mean a couple of dirty magazines under their beds. I mean they can watch virtually anything they want on their smartphones without anyone knowing about it.

By the grace of God, as a freshman in high school, I was introduced to a ministry called Young Life. Young Life is a Christian outreach ministry focused on building relationships with high school kids and earning the right to be heard. Where my parents and youth group pastors avoided conversations about purity, my Young Life leaders were willing to talk about it. My best friends and I started attending Campaigners, a weekly Bible study. Our Young Life leaders, who were in their early twenties, became a sounding board for all our "gray area" questions. I felt like I could trust them, which made it easier to ask awkward or embarrassing questions about everything that fell between holding hands and having sex.

During one of our Sunday evening Campaigners meetings, one of my leaders used a visual—a pink paper heart glued to a blue paper heart—to convey the serious consequences of sexual pleasure outside of marriage. She held up the pink side and said, "This is what your heart looks like when you protect your purity." Then she started to peel away the blue heart from the pink heart and said, "And here's what can happen when you don't." As she pulled the hearts apart, remnants of the blue heart stuck to the pink heart, and there were chunks of the pink heart stuck to the blue heart. The pink heart was also thinner and more fragile than before. It was the first time I really understood the ramifications of physical intimacy outside of marriage. It put a whole new perspective on Proverbs 4:23 (NLT): "Guard your heart above all else, for it determines the course of your life." My Young Life leader went on to encourage us to pursue purity so we would one day be able to give our whole heart to our future spouse.

Looking back, I still consider it a powerful illustration, but it also had at least two unintended and negative ramifications. The first was that it left my friends who had already slept with their boyfriends feeling overwhelming shame and guilt. It made them feel as if their heart would never be whole again, which is not true. I had a conversation with one friend who said, "Well, I've already messed up, and since I don't have a whole heart to give anyway, there's no point in fighting for purity now." If this is you, let these words from Mary Pickford sink in: "You may have a fresh start any moment you choose, for this thing that we call 'failure' is not the falling down, but the staying down."[1] When it comes to purity, you can choose the fresh start too.

The second negative consequence of the paper heart analogy is that it limits the purpose of purity to one's unknown future spouse rather than casting the broader vision of purity as God's designed path for sexuality. A purity ring should not symbolize a promise to someone you don't even know yet; it should symbolize a promise to your heavenly Father, your Savior, your Redeemer, the one who knows all the ways you've messed up and yet loves you completely and calls you to a better way. A purity ring should be a reminder to receive God's promises and believe that his way is the most blessed path. That's why God's Word cautions us to not "arouse or awaken love until it so desires" (Song of Songs 8:4). In other words, don't initiate the sexual part of your relationship until you can pursue it.

If you're reading this and you feel like your purity is lost or ruined, please hear this. God's grace makes the purity battle not about what you did with your body but about what he did with his. If you repent, forgiveness is yours, purity is yours, wholeness is yours. The Bible often refers to God as our Redeemer (for example, Isaiah 47:4). He redeems our brokenness and makes us pure again. Redemption is an invitation from confinement to freedom, from anxiety to peace, from shame to dignity, from addiction to self-control, from selfishness to servanthood, from depression to joy, from complacency to growth, from disobedience to honor, and from sickness to health. Our Redeemer God wants to make you a new creation (2 Corinthians 5:17). He wants to create a pure heart in you and renew a steadfast spirit within you (Psalm 51:10). And in case you're hearing this for the first time, I need to make one thing clear. There is nothing you or I can do to earn this gift of grace. We simply get to receive it and allow it to transform our lives.

* * *

When I was growing up, my parents didn't let my siblings and me eat much candy or sugar, except on birthdays or holidays, and even then, it was usually a homemade cake or fresh berry pie. So of course, whenever I went over to my friends' houses, I ate my fill of Gushers, Fruit by the Foot, and Costco muffins—all of which were banned in the Botti household. I was the classic junk food–deprived kid who binged when given the opportunity. When you're a kid and someone says you can't have something, you always end up wanting it more, even when you know overindulging will make you sick.

In the same way that not being allowed to have junk food only intensified my craving for it, not being able to kiss Jeremy for months at a time made me want to do more than kiss him when we were finally together. Additionally, we discovered that the anticipation of not seeing each other for long periods of time created a lot of sexual tension when we were together. If you've ever been in a long-distance relationship, this will resonate with you. When you've only seen the person you love via a cell phone screen for three months, it's a lot harder to keep your hands off each other when you're finally together.

Long distance kept the candy jar out of reach, but when Jeremy and I were together, we had the freedom to indulge, and our sweet tooth was strong. But every time we gave in to our cravings and compromised our values, we always felt sick with guilt and shame afterward. Admittedly, making out was our shortcut to feeling emotionally connected again after long periods of not seeing each other. Physical intimacy was an easy way to reassure one another that the chemistry was still there. It was affirming in the moment, but we knew it was outside of God's will and against his ways. We felt so weak and pathetic for not having enough self-discipline to control ourselves.

The few times I visited Jeremy in Santa Barbara, I usually stayed with one of his female church friends. However, during one of my visits, everyone was out of town for the holiday, and I ended up staying at Jeremy's house. *Not* ideal. I pep-talked myself into thinking we would be fine because Jer lived with three other dudes, and I wasn't about to be all PDA around them. Plus, I was only there for two nights.

My first night in town was the Fourth of July, and we rode our bikes to the beach to watch a fireworks show. We got caught up in the romance of the scene and slipped away from the spectators to steal a few lingering kisses. It's no surprise that kissing on the beach aroused our desire for more physical connection when we got back to Jer's house. I know it's taboo for Christian couples to talk about this kind of stuff, but I'm not going to lie or sugarcoat what happened.

Back in Jer's room, we did more than make out. We drew a hard line at sex, but we definitely entered the gray area. To make matters worse, I was wearing my swimsuit because that's what you do in Santa Barbara. But this made it seem much more acceptable for me to slip off my dress as things got steamy. At the precise moment I did this, the alarm on my phone went off. We froze and backed away from each other with raised eyebrows and clenched-teeth smiles. I had set the alarm intentionally, and it was effective.

My mom used to always say, "Nothing good happens after midnight." However, based on our history, I knew that 10 p.m. was usually the time when we would return from our evening adventure and face a choice: go home or start a late-night movie, campfire, or conversation. The latter choices always tempted us sexually. My college mentor Jamie suggested that I set an alarm for 10 p.m. as an accountability measure. She knew I was staying with Jer that weekend and thought it might be a good way to set me up for success in the purity department.

Shortly after my alarm reminded me to make the disciplined choice, I got a text from Jamie. Hey, Auj, just holding you accountable here. You in your own bed?

I didn't want to tell her I wasn't, so I immediately said good night to Jer and got ready for bed, while Jer climbed into the pile of blankets on the floor so I could reply back. Yes (insert embarrassed emoji face).

But don't think I got off the hook so easily. When I returned from my visit, Jamie asked me more pointed questions, and I had to disclose the details of how we'd messed up. Yes, it was embarrassing and awkward, but it was also completely necessary. She spoke the hard truth I needed to hear and helped me brainstorm additional ways Jer and I could set boundaries and accountability measures moving forward.

To demonstrate just how hard the purity battle was for us, the next night we fell prey to the same trap. I'm telling you, we *burned*! If we had been this much in love a century ago, nothing would have prevented us from getting married at this point. But it wasn't a hundred years ago, and we were bound by other pressures and goals—to complete college degrees, have stable incomes, and plan a Pinterest-worthy wedding. So we "waited."

The second night of my visit, we were watching a movie while cuddling on Jer's bed late at night—a recipe for disaster. This time, it wasn't my alarm that stopped us, but Jeremy. He offered a creative yet slightly laughable solution. "Auj, I'm getting in my sleeping bag, and I'm not coming out till morning. You can sleep in my bed cause it's more comfy. Good night!"

I slept under the covers, and Jer slept on top of the covers in his sleeping bag. By the way, this is not something I condone *at all*, but I'm just trying to be real here. We struggled. Sometime early in the morning, I must have rolled over and ended up kicking Jer's sleeping bag. The slippery material caused him to slide right off the bed, and we both woke up laughing hysterically.

I share all of this to acknowledge the reality of how hard it is to fight this fight. Being extremely attracted to someone you love but aren't married to doesn't make it easy. The media doesn't make it easy. Chick flicks don't make it easy. Your own college bedroom doesn't make it easy. The wedding industry doesn't make it easy. A purity ring doesn't make it easy. And long distance certainly doesn't make it easy. To fight for purity, we need to protect ourselves with accountability and boundaries.

JEREMY

When I first met Audrey, I was failing behind the computer screen. I had wandering eyes when it came to risqué images and social media profiles I had no business looking at. I know many men who excuse their porn habit because there is no nudity, but the sin of porn can happen in the mind with or without articles of clothing, no matter whether it's on an Instagram feed or an explicit website. We're told in Scripture that we will give an account for all our thoughts and actions. When we meet Jesus face-to-face and give an account for our entire life, I don't think that when it comes to our viewing habits, he'll say, "Oh, well at least they were barely clothed so your thoughts were okay." Scripture tells us God "will bring to light what is hidden in darkness and will expose the motives of the heart" (1 Corinthians 4:5).

Then came Audrey, and I felt a new sense of conviction. In my heart, I felt that my eyes and purity were meant for her. God definitely used Audrey to wake me up. I began to evaluate who I was becoming, and discerned that my actions were inconsistent with the man I aspired to be—a man of maturity, discipline, and self-control. I've heard it said that the true mark of a man is whether he can control himself. If a man cannot control his own mind, he'll never be able to control his own actions.

I began pursuing Audrey and wouldn't look at anything risqué for weeks at a time. But sure enough, every month or so, I'd get lazy, bored, or stressed and find myself scrolling in places I shouldn't be. Afterward I always felt gross and disappointed in myself. My spirit felt off, and I hated that I kept doing it (Romans 7:13–20).

Desperate to find a solution, I picked up *Mere Christianity* by C. S. Lewis—another book that changed my life. Lewis makes the case that our morals—our standards of right and wrong—come directly from God. Morals are not simply social mores created *by* human beings, but rather they are standards created by God *for* human beings. Lewis likens morals to a type of fuel. God built the human machine, and he designed us to operate in a certain way, on a specific fuel.[2] When we choose to run on any other kind of fuel, such as the standards of a peer group or the wider culture, we'll eventually break down. Which is exactly what happens when you put the wrong kind of fuel in a car—put diesel in a nondiesel motor, and you're in trouble. If we decide to run our lives on anything other than the fuel our Creator designed for us, we're in trouble.

Fortunately, we have free will and get to choose the fuel we run on. Christians who use porn know it's not the right fuel, and so in making the choice to use it, we willingly contradict our beliefs with our actions. I realized I was a hypocrite. I said I believed one thing but acted out another in secret, and I was breaking down, whether or not I recognized it.

Speaking from experience, I've noticed that people often misdiagnose themselves concerning things they can't seem to quit. We won't admit we're actually addicted, and so we say things like, "I can stop whenever I want" or "I can take care of the problem myself." Then weeks turn into months, or even years. And at that point, we're trapped, ashamed, disconnected, and totally out of fellowship with the Lord.

In *The Power of Habit*, author Charles Duhigg describes what he calls a bad habit loop as the gateway to addiction. The primary difference between a habit loop and an addiction is that a person controls the habit, but an addiction controls the person. Duhigg states that every addiction starts out as a habit, and every habit runs on the same cycle: cue, routine, reward.[3] There is a cue, such as stress or boredom. There is a routine, such as searching certain kinds of profiles on social media. And there is a reward, such as excitement or arousal. This was my habit loop for years.

On many occasions, I was able to withstand the temptation and get clean, but at some point, I ended up back in the same pit. Duhigg's book helped me understand why, at least in part: while I succeeded in breaking my habit loop, I failed to replace it with something else. For example, I stopped looking at images of half-naked women, which was my routine, but that didn't stop my mind from getting bored and desiring a reward. If we fail to replace our routine with something else that gives us a reward, we're doomed to fall back into the same old habit loops.

All habits are a cycle—cue, routine, reward. What we need to do is replace our old routine with a new one. For me, it was push-ups. When I found myself sitting around at home alone and boredom started to creep in (cue), I'd pick up my phone to entertain myself, which sometimes led to viewing provocative images (old routine). Instead, I did a few sets of push-ups (new routine) and in turn felt stimulated and got a testosterone boost (reward). I'd then move on to whatever I should've been doing.

This worked great, and I went a year being able to uphold a healthy respect for women and protecting my purity. However, the parasitical sin had not vanished, and during the stress following our wedding, I fell back into my old habit loop—cue, routine, reward. It wasn't until we moved to Bend, Oregon, in our second year of marriage, that I identified the foundational failure behind my failure to kill the sin: I had been trying to overcome my addiction on my own.

In Bend, Auj and I got plugged into a house church, which is simply a small group of Christians who meet in a private home. This group became our community—the people we did life with in an intentional way. It was here that I found a pastor who wouldn't stand for unrepented, habitual sin. He called me out and set me straight as he explained the biblical truths about someone who refuses to turn from sin and walk in righteousness.

In the context of intentional community, I realized how isolated I was in my efforts to change and grow, so I started meeting with the guys from the group. These were the kind of godly men I aspired to become. They knew the Word, challenged one another, and loved the "iron sharpening iron" process that Proverbs 27:17 refers to. We had found a community of believers who not only believed the Word of God but were determined to live it out, no matter how costly or countercultural it was.

When we keep sin in the dark, guess what—it stays there. The apostle Paul describes the Christian life as a long-distance race, one in which "all athletes are disciplined in their training" and "run with purpose in every step" (1 Corinthians 9:25–26 NLT). For most of my life, I've ignored training and gotten away with just winging it—like when I decided to take my SAT test without any preparation, learned to drive a stick shift while driving OhSo home for the first time, or decided on the morning of the race to run a half marathon.

Winging it with my faith, however, only left me with a weakness in my character, one that wasn't fully addressed until a man called me out and I pursued the accountability of other Christian men. God never intended the Christian race to be run alone. In community, I finally had the support of people who loved me and would not let me fail, people who cared more for my soul than my comfort. And it was their support that finally gave me the courage to confess my struggles to Audrey.

I had come to terms that there was no "convenient" time to

approach Audrey, so I decided to bring it up on a Sunday evening during our weekly marriage journal session we call Navigator's Council.[4] My demeanor changed when we got to this question: *Is there any unconfessed sin, conflict, or hurt that we need to resolve or seek forgiveness for?*

I began the humbling process of confessing my sin and asking Audrey for forgiveness. When I saw the look of betrayal in her eyes, I felt mournfully sorry. Tears ran down her beautiful face.

"Why, Jer?" she asked. "Why?"

I didn't have an answer. The only words that came out of my mouth were, "I don't know," which didn't help the situation.

Audrey was devastated. My behavior had fractured our trust, scarred our intimacy, and broken our unity. I remember thinking, *I love her so much. Why do I keep doing this?* Yes, I loved her, but to what extent? We show our love for others by how we treat them. So if I said I loved her but chose to do something that hurt her, there's a discrepancy there that I needed to reckon with.

I repented to the Lord and promised Audrey I would have eyes only for her. To repent means to "turn away from"—to "go now and leave your life of sin" (John 8:11). Being made new and washed clean, I turned from my old ways and into freedom. After apologizing to Audrey and getting my darkness into the light, I was set free—again. Only this time I had the backing of Christian accountability. It's for difficult and painful issues such as this that the Christian walk is meant to be done alongside fellow believers. God uses Christian community to encourage and comfort, but also to convict, correct, and cure. If you're struggling in the dark, give it up! Walking the road to freedom and purity is difficult, but the Bible is clear that the rewards of being alive in Christ and dead to sin will be worth whatever it takes to do it.

AUDREY

If you're currently in a dating relationship, ask yourself, *Am I and my boyfriend [girlfriend] both committed to pursuing purity and waiting until marriage?* It can't be a solo fight. You'll never win if you don't have the same end goal—pursuing God's design for sex and physical intimacy. The apostle Paul writes, "It is God's will that you should be sanctified: that you should avoid sexual immorality; that each of you should learn to control your own body in a way that is holy and honorable, not in passionate lust like the pagans, who do not know God" (1 Thessalonians 4:3–5).

When it comes to sexual temptation outside of marriage, God is pretty clear on his instruction: Don't walk; run. First Corinthians 6:18–20 reads, "Flee from sexual immorality. All other sins a person commits are outside the body, but whoever sins sexually, sins against their own body . . . You are not your own; you were bought at a price. Therefore honor God with your bodies."

God gave us sexual desires to be enjoyed within the confines of marriage. His Word says, "It is not good for the man to be alone," that "it is better to marry than to burn with passion," and that "the two will become one flesh" (Genesis 2:18; 1 Corinthians 7:9; Mark 10:8). And guess what, the Bible tells us *not* to refrain from sex *within* marriage. First Corinthians 7:5 reads, "Do not deprive each other except perhaps by mutual consent and for a time, so that you may devote yourselves to prayer. Then come together again, so that Satan will not tempt you because of your lack of self-control."

Notice the verse does not demand sex, but rather encourages married couples not to rob each other from experiencing the sexual pleasure God designed for us to enjoy as husband and wife. We're not to withhold sex as a means of exercising power or proving a point. God wants us to experience the fullness of his joy and eternal pleasures (Psalm 16:11). The boundaries he gives us surrounding purity and sex are designed to elevate and enhance sexual pleasure, not to chasten and curtail it.

That's the kind of husband or wife you can trust with your heart for the rest of your life. If the person you're dating won't honor and respect God's design for purity now, what makes you think he or she will honor and respect God's design for sex within marriage?

To all of you boyfriends or girlfriends out there, if your dating relationship is headed toward marriage, I encourage you to begin asking each other some hard questions:

- Do you desire to wait for marriage?
- How were you raised to view purity?
- Have you been sexually intimate in a previous relationship?
- Have you ever looked at porn?
- If so, when was the last time?
- Do you have people in your life holding you accountable to resist this temptation?

If you're already married but have never had these kinds of conversations with your spouse, please start now.

Recent studies consistently indicate that more than 70 percent of men ages eighteen to twenty-four view porn at least once a week, and those are just the guys who are willing to admit it. If you're dating a man with a pornography struggle or addiction, it is *not* your job to help him overcome it. He needs help outside of your relationship. If he is serious about overcoming this issue, he will prove it through accountability with other faithful men who are not struggling with the same sin. Guys with porn addictions cannot hold other guys with porn addictions accountable.

This is also true for women struggling with this sin.

So if you find out your boyfriend, girlfriend, fiancé, fiancée, husband, or wife has a porn addiction or is struggling with this habitual sin, what should you do? There are no easy or one-size-fits-all answers, but asking yourself a few questions may help you identify whether you should break things off:

- Am I confident in his or her sincere commitment to overcoming this sin?
- What evidence do I have that he or she takes this issue seriously?
- Does he or she have accountability from mentors and friends who are *not* wrestling with the same sin?

I'm currently walking with a close friend who married a guy who secretly struggled with porn throughout their dating relationship and into their marriage. Over the years, dabbling in porn became an addiction, and the addiction ultimately led to an affair that shattered two hearts and left four young children confused and hurting. My friend knew her husband had some struggles, but she never thought things would get to the point that he'd have an affair.

I've heard it said that the only thing that keeps a boyfriend who watches pornography from becoming a husband who commits adultery is the right opportunity. And the biblical standard for what constitutes adultery is pretty high. Jesus said, "You have heard that it was said, 'You shall not commit adultery.' But I tell you that anyone who looks at a woman lustfully has already committed adultery with her in his heart" (Matthew 5:27–28).

Long before smartphones and social media amplified the porn epidemic of today, Jesus made a direct connection between lust and adultery. And it's not hard to make a similar connection between the porn industry and adultery. Friend, don't drag a porn addiction, or even a porn struggle, into your marriage. The effects on your marriage will be nothing but destructive. We experienced them during the first year of our marriage, and I wouldn't wish that kind of heartache on anyone.

If not dealt with, sexual impurity before marriage becomes sexual impurity in marriage. If you blur the lines while dating, who's to say you won't blur the lines while married? Sex is supposed to be a beautifully unifying act of oneness, but if sex occurs in conjunction with a porn addiction, or in the context of a partner who fantasizes about another man or woman during lovemaking, then the unifying part of sex is nullified. This strips sex down to a selfish act. It depletes sex of the pleasure, connection, and resolve it was designed to offer within the context of marriage.

I like to assume no one sets out to have an affair, yet every affair starts with two people who, having proclaimed their love for one another on their wedding day, ultimately failed to protect that love with boundaries, commitment, accountability, and honesty. It's heartbreaking. And being a Christian doesn't grant you immunity from "the sin that so easily entangles" (Hebrews 12:1). We cannot be so naive to think, *Oh, I'm better than that. It will never happen to me. I can handle it.* These delusional justifications are what keep us walking the line between sin and holiness.

No one sins on accident. We sin because we're walking the line. In dating and marriage relationships, we shouldn't be asking, *Where is the line and how close can I get to it?* We should be asking, *If there is a line, how far away can I stay from it? How wholeheartedly can I pursue purity? How can I keep my eyes from wandering? How can I have eyes solely for my spouse?* Wrestling with these kinds of questions will help us establish boundaries so we can win the purity battle before and after we say, "I do."

PRACTICAL BOUNDARIES
FOR DATING COUPLES

Here are a few practical boundaries and accountability measures that helped us fight for purity during our dating relationship and in the days leading up to "I do." We hope that what we learned from our failures will set you up for success.

- When you are alone, leave the door open.
- Set an alarm for when you will say good-bye for the night.
- Trust the wisdom of people who have "been there, done that."
- Find a friend or mentor who will hold you accountable and tell this person when you will be spending time with your boyfriend or girlfriend.
- If you're wrestling with the sin of pornography, find a mentor or accountability partner who does not struggle with the same sin. Then set other practical boundaries, such as installing monitoring or blocking programs on computers, phones, and other devices, as well as pledging not to use your phone late at night or in bed.
- Make the people in your life aware of your desire to wait for marriage.
- Don't lie down together when watching movies.
- Don't watch movies with nudity when together—or when separate, for that matter.
- Be aware of how you are dressed and keep it modest.

And if you're in a long-distance relationship . . .

- Decide in advance where you're going to sleep or stay, which should ideally be with a friend at a separate location.
- Don't sleep on the floor in his or her room.
- Let a friend or mentor know when you are visiting and ask this person to hold you accountable throughout your visit and to talk with you about the visit afterward.

Don't let our culture's devaluation of purity tempt you to deviate from God's way. Have the awkward conversations, set up boundaries, and run away from the line. Whether you're single, dating, engaged, or married, the purity battle is one you'll likely fight for the rest of your life. And the battle is only growing more monstrous with the increasing accessibility of porn, the rise of sex and nudity in TV and movies, the growing percentage of workplace affairs, the ease of secretly communicating with a friend of the opposite sex, the decline of modesty, and the ability to escape to an alternate world at the palm of your hands.

I don't say this to discourage you, but rather to emphasize the importance of arming yourself with protection for the battlefield. The good news is, God gives us full armor (Ephesians 6) to be more than overcomers (Romans 8:37). Be confident and encouraged that you are fighting for God's way, and his ways are higher than our ways (Isaiah 55:9). His design for purity before and within marriage is for our good and his glory. When we choose to live into his design, it is pleasurable, fruitful, exciting, full of joy, breathtakingly beautiful, and worth it. Remember God's promise. When you are tempted, he will always show you a way out (1 Corinthians 10:13). So when you see the light shining into your darkness, run toward it. Keep fighting the good fight, finish the race, and keep the faith (2 Timothy 4:7).

THE BIG
QUESTION

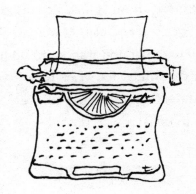

JEREMY

It had been more than two years since I asked Audrey to date me before I left to attend the Brooks Institute in Santa Barbara, and now I was finishing up my last year of school. Audrey was set to graduate in June, and I would graduate just two months later in August. We had already been talking about our plans after graduation, including marriage. We weren't going to be one of those couples who couldn't commit. In fact, I think we would have been married a year before if distance hadn't gotten in the way. Our relationship wasn't perfect, and neither were we, but we loved each other, worked well together and wanted to do life alongside each other. I remember that time a few years back in my mom's kitchen when I proclaimed that I would marry Audrey. Now the time had come. I was ready to marry this girl!

*　*　*

High-rise office buildings towered over my friend Tye and me as we crept through traffic in downtown Los Angeles on our way to the Jewelry District—a collection of 5,000 jewelry stores contained within six city blocks. When I couldn't seem to find an engagement ring that suited Audrey, I had decided to design my own. A friend had hooked me up with a custom jeweler who said she could make me a ring.

Passing an armed guard, we entered our destination and approached the front desk. The receptionist told us the office we were looking for was on the fifth floor and pointed to the stairs. Short-winded after hiking up five flights, we opened the door to the fifth floor and approached door 504. After a few deep breaths and a nod of affirmation from Tye, I knocked on the door, and we walked in.

The "office" was the size of a closet. Not kidding. It was literally five feet wide and just barely deep enough to open the door all the way. In fact, the door hit the backs of two chairs as we opened it. In front of the chairs was a counter and a thick Plexiglas wall that rose to the ceiling. Apprehension struck immediately. *We must have made a mistake.* This was definitely not looking like the ring-designing experience I had imagined.

After we'd stood there for a few minutes, a young woman came hurriedly from around the corner and greeted us through the holes in the glass. Her demeanor was warm and reassuring, and I relaxed a little. A few moments later, we were joined by the woman's father. Evidently, this was a family business, and I liked that.

We discussed my vision and what I wanted in a ring—something timeless and unique, just like our love story. Oh, and I wanted to engrave the words "Braid it" on the inside. In one of my poems to Audrey, I'd written, "May we braid it together, Christ, you, and I." The line is a reference to a Scripture verse that reads, "A person standing alone can be attacked and defeated, but two can stand back-to-back and conquer. Three are even better, for a triple-braided cord is not easily broken" (Ecclesiastes 4:12 NLT). Christ is the third strand who prevents the unraveling. "Braid it" was our reminder that strong relationships have a three-strand structure, and we wanted that structure for the slogan of our love—plus, it's a play on Daisy Braids, my nickname for Audrey.

```
               To our future ahead
                may it ever be met
      Let us draw our compass in the hands of Christ
           May no trial collect its due
     Lord, grant us the strength to pursue on through
        May we braid it together, Christ, you, and I
       And let us build upon this contagious love
           Our past behind may we never forget
                        Amen
                       JEREMY
```

After I handed over a wad of cash, the woman behind the Plexiglas said she would give me a call in a few weeks when the ring was ready.

Now all I had to do was decide how to propose. This proved to be more difficult than I had expected. As the weeks went by, the pressure to make it perfect mounted. Instead of getting closer to having a plan, I was getting farther away from one. One evening, I was talking about it with a friend, and he could see my distress. "Jer, you're unique, and so is your love story," he said. "Whatever you do, just make it a reflection of your story. If you do that, it'll be fine." *Ah! Why didn't I think of that? Our story—of course!* Almost immediately, I had a plan.

The trestle. It had to be at the trestle. It was at the trestle that I first pushed the envelope of our relationship from friendship to dating. It was at the trestle that I asked Audrey to officially date me. It was at the trestle that we got back together after our breakup. And now it would be at the trestle that I would ask her to marry me.

Here's how it went down.

I flew home to Portland with the ring in my pocket—yes, I checked it for holes—and the typewriter in my bag. It was mid-March—Audrey's spring break—and I would be in Portland for one of my two-week breaks. That was just enough time to finalize the details of my plan, propose, and revel in the glory before heading back to Santa Barbara.

Upon my arrival at the farm, I went straight to the garage and made sure Rain was still willing to start for me. Sure enough, she fired right up! I drove down to the trestle to map out where it would all take place. The spring rains had begun, making the pathway and field alongside the trestle muddy but still manageable. The forecast for the week ahead was clear skies, so I decided to wait a few days for the ground to dry out a little. This actually worked out for the better because I had some other plans in the works that took longer to arrange than I expected. Regardless, rain or shine, I would still propose!

A few days later, Audrey came home from school for the weekend. I told her I wanted to have a picnic at the trestle. I knew she wouldn't suspect anything because a picnic wasn't out of the ordinary. Plus, we hadn't been to the trestle for a while, so it seemed fitting. A few days earlier, I had also attempted to throw her off course by saying we should talk about the ring situation so I could start looking. All of which is to say, I was pretty sure my proposal would be a complete surprise!

On March 15, 2014, I hopped into Rain and picked up Audrey from her parents' house. She came out wearing her muck boots, as I'd asked her to. I felt numb—totally frozen all over. Like I was breathing water and my blood was liquid cement. Every movement felt forced and unnatural.

On our way to the trestle, I realized I was running early, so I decided to head back to the farm to buy some time. Audrey was slightly confused at first, but I recovered by telling her I needed to grab some picnic supplies I had forgotten. I had to keep my cool under pressure—which wasn't easy.

When I finally got the text, We're good, I casually suggested we head to the trestle. I thought for sure the whole thing felt fishy, but Audrey seemed to be clueless. We loaded back into Rain and drove down to the trestle. It felt like everything I did was so obvious. *I'm sure she can hear my heartbeat. Does she notice how trembly my voice is? I wonder if she thinks I'm acting weird.* We parked alongside the road and began walking toward the trestle.

I led her out into the field a little ways and laid out a blanket. Not knowing what to do and afraid to waste too much time, I pulled the typewriter from my bag and loaded a piece of paper into the roller. Beginning to type, I looked over at Audrey and smiled. She smiled back. I wanted to marry this girl—there was no doubt.

We took turns typing out a list of all the ways we could love each other:

1. Commit to a weekly Navigator's Council session.[1]
2. Jer doesn't always have to be right.
3. Spend intentional morning time with Jesus.
4. Acknowledge each other's point of view in public.
5. Be aware.

When we felt like we had a good list, I said, "I've got one last one!"

I grabbed the typewriter from Auj and turned it around so she couldn't see what I was typing. I felt like I was going to pass out from the adrenaline. I felt like my brain was losing control over my motor skills. Turning the typewriter back around, I placed it in her lap.

```
Speaking of marriage, Audrey Mirabella Botti, will you
marry me?
```

By the time she lifted her head and met my gaze, I had the ring in my hand and was on one knee so I could ask her again, this time with my voice.

"Audrey, will you marry me?"

"Yes!" she said, and she wrapped her arms around me.

A few moments later, I gave the whistle to alert my two friends that it was all right to come out. They had been hiding in the bushes with cameras to capture the moment. If you're wondering how you saw our proposal episode on *Little People, Big World*, it's because I later gave the footage to TLC.

In relief and shock, we talked about what had just happened before heading up to the trestle in order to "lock it in" with a few photos.

The Big Question was a storybook success!

8

PREPARING
for the Promise

AUDREY

Jeremy and I had talked about getting married after we both graduated, so I had been anticipating his proposal for about a year. I knew it was coming; I just wasn't sure when. However, as Christmas, New Year's, and Valentine's Day passed, I started to wonder if he even had a ring or a plan to propose. It wasn't unlike him to procrastinate, but I was getting a little anxious as the summer drew closer. I wanted to have enough time to find a dreamy dress and plan an epic celebration. I became the cliché girl anxiously waiting for "a ring by spring." But Jeremy was not cliché, and he was not about to ask me to marry him on a holiday like all the other guys did. I should have known better. March 15 was perfect.

When I returned to school after Jer's beautiful proposal, I caught myself constantly glancing down at my sparkling ring and showing it off any chance I got. I was ecstatic to finally be a fiancée and thought I could put the anxiety of waiting behind me. But now instead of worrying about when he was going to propose, I was worrying about everything else—applying for jobs, finding wedding vendors, passing my finance class, competing in my last season of collegiate track and field, and preparing for graduation.

We ended up having the most stressful engagement imaginable. Planning a wedding while living in different states was brutal. Plus, we were both trying to establish our career paths and decide where we wanted to live. I ended up accepting a corporate sales job in Los Angeles. I had been applying for jobs there, since that's where most of Jeremy's video and photo opportunities were. By the grace of God, I was able to delay my start date until the week after our wedding.

Throughout the summer, we were searching for a place to live in LA, which is a daunting task all by itself, but especially so when neither of us lived there. Jeremy had to make the two-hour drive from Santa Barbara multiple times to meet with landlords in the hopes that we would be picked from the large number of applicants. I flew down once to search with him. If you've ever looked for a place to live in a big city, you know it's worse than Black Friday shopping at the mall.

On top of all this, Jeremy was taking a heavy load of classes and filming weddings on the weekends with his friend Tye. Other summer commitments included planning our honeymoon, partic-ipating in my best friend's wedding, taking a group of high school Young Life girls to camp in Canada, buying our first car (which I needed for my new job), and my parents selling the house I grew up in (where I was temporarily living). I moved three times that summer. Oh, and did I mention that our entire engagement and wedding planning process was also being filmed for *Little People, Big World*? Looking back on it now, I can't believe we got through it without damaging repercussions. It was a turbulent season, for sure, but we were committed to preparing for the promise—and that's what kept us steadfast on the voyage.

Despite our whirlwind of applying, searching, packing, and planning, we were adamant about prioritizing our future promise. We were committed to preparing more for our marriage than our wedding. We didn't want all of our planning for the big day to defeat the purpose of the big day. That's a temptation we considered low-hanging fruit for the enemy. We weren't about to let Satan try to sabotage our future union.

In the Bible, Satan is referred to as an accuser and our adversary. He wants to separate what God wants to join together. He is against marriage. He wants to create division, strife, and drama where God wants to instill unity, peace, and oneness. We were not immune to enemy attacks during our season of engagement. We experienced conflict with our parents, frustrations related to long distance, denials of housing applications, lost job opportunities, drama while filming the television show, and some hard and hurtful conversations with each other. However, we fought back against the onslaught of attacks on our future promise with an unrelenting confidence that the enemy would not be able to separate what the Lord was joining together.

* * *

Before I dive into some practical ways we protected our love and prepared for our marriage, may I first talk about kindergarten friendships? I promise I have a point.

Remember how you made friends when you were five? It probably went something like this. At recess, you discovered that

Sara's favorite playground activity was also the tire swing, or during lunch you noticed that Kyle had the same Superman lunch box. These commonalities were enough to make you instant besties. When you're a kid, you don't really choose your friends; they sort of just happen to you. In kindergarten, friendships come easily—but they also go easily. One week you're swinging together at recess and pinky promising that you'll be best friends forever, and the next week you've moved on and are doing the same thing all over again with someone new. Sound familiar?

Unfortunately, this expectation that relationships just happen doesn't end in kindergarten. Our generation is being fed a false doctrine about love. The media of today have most of us believing that love is serendipitous—something that happens by chance. They've portrayed love as merely an emotion that we fall into and out of. All of this has made us so infatuated with "falling in love" that we've lost sight of what love really is—a choice, a verb, a commitment, a promise.

Love that lasts isn't something we can easily fall in and out of. Nor is it something that just happens to us. Love that lasts is an unconditional pursuit full of uncompromising sacrifices. All this to say, choosing the person you will love for the rest of your life is the most pervasively life-altering decision you will ever make. It will influence everything—from your work, home, family, and finances to how you endure heartache and experience joy. The magnitude of this decision merits the accountability, encouragement, and "iron sharpening iron" experience that only comes from other couples who have been there and done that. On our journey to "I do," Jeremy and I were intentional about seeking out wise counsel.

Premarital counseling was one of the most impactful things we did to prepare for the promise. We knew it would be challenging to pull off logistically because we were living in different states, but that wasn't going to stop us. Conveniently, my college mentor, Jamie Herb, and her husband, Chris, were premarital counselors, so we asked if they would counsel us. Chris and Jamie had met Jeremy a few times when he had come to visit me in Corvallis, but mostly they knew him through me. Both Jeremy and I deeply admired and respected their marriage. In addition to doing our premarital counseling, we also wanted Chris to officiate our wedding. When the time came, they eagerly agreed.

At our first session, Chris and Jamie got us started by sharing their life stories, and then Jeremy and I fumbled our way through ours. It was surprisingly enlightening to hear each other talk about the moments, relationships, and circumstances that had shaped us most. It was also the first time Jer and I had formally shared with each other how we came to our faith. Of course, we knew bits and pieces of each other's life stories, but there was something powerful about hearing them in a chronological way.

In each subsequent session, we talked through a topic, such as spiritual life, family, communication, finances, and physical intimacy. Chris and Jamie began by offering their wisdom and encouragement and pointing out Scriptures to support what they shared. Then they asked us questions to get us thinking more deeply and talking about how we envisioned these aspects of our life together.

In our discussion about our spiritual life, we talked about keeping Christ at the center of our marriage and seeking him first, even before each other. We talked about living into our marital roles, equal in value but different in nature. We studied what the Bible has to say about the marriage covenant. In our conversations after this session, Jer and I were eager to talk about implementing the principle of sharing in a way that would allow a covenant mind-set to flourish within our marriage.

When you become one on your wedding day, you enter into a covenant relationship the Bible describes as becoming "one flesh" (Genesis 2:24). Living this out entails making choices that reflect and honor your covenant beyond the wedding day. That's what it means to have a covenant mind-set. It requires total commitment. There is no plan B. You are all in—100 percent, no matter what. When you have a covenant mind-set, you're willing to do and to sacrifice whatever it takes to make it work.

A covenant mind-set is not a contract but a promise, one that was modeled for us by Jesus. Through Jesus' death on the cross, he established a covenant with us (Luke 22:20; Hebrews 7:22; 9:15). To draw a parallel, entering into the covenant of marriage also requires a death, specifically, a death to self. This doesn't mean we become doormats; it means we make an empowered choice to love sacrificially, just as Jesus did. A covenant mind-set reflects our promise to love each other completely, "as long as we both shall live." Because it is a promise (unconditional) rather than a contract (conditional), a covenant mind-set says, "Even if you won't, I still will." It's a mind-set that believes "for better, for worse" and esteems holiness above happiness.

In one of our premarital counseling sessions, we discussed what our parents had modeled to us about spiritual life, and we determined what we wanted to follow after and what we wanted to fight against. Some of these conversations carried over into our later sessions about family and communication. We talked about how our parents shaped our view of marriage and about their differing styles of communication.

For example, I grew up in a family that was very verbal. It was a constant speech and debate class in the Botti household. All of us had strong opinions we weren't afraid to share, often with raised voices. We saw no need to hide our emotions or to pretend that everything was okay when it wasn't. My parents never hid their conflicts from us. We saw them fight, and we also saw them reconcile.

The Roloff family's communication style was pretty much the opposite. Jeremy rarely saw his parents fight. Whenever he got in trouble or got in a fight with his parents, it usually expressed itself in a passive-aggressive way that ended with him running off to his fort or being sent to his room. Rather than discussing and resolving conflict, he developed a habit of stuffing and avoiding it, of "numbing out."

The Herbs warned us that our differing communication styles had the potential to create frustration and bitterness. I was used to talking things out, and Jer was used to walking away. Knowing this helped us be more aware of the pitfalls when we encountered conflict. We learned that I would need to give Jeremy space when I sensed he needed it, and Jeremy would need to engage conflict with an aim to resolve it rather than escape it. As we talked about our communication styles, Chris and Jamie offered some practical tips for preventing conflict. They urged us to communicate our needs, affirm each other in front of our friends, avoid sarcasm, eliminate the words *never* and *always* from our vocabulary, make our expectations known, and pray for each other daily.

In our discussion about finances, we talked through our families' financial histories and how we were raised to view and use money. Jeremy and I shared our history and habits when it came to debt, saving, investing, giving, budgeting, and spending. This helped us devise a plan to steward our resources well as we embraced "joint checking."

First, we discussed debt. Jeremy and I felt incredibly blessed to be entering into our marriage without student loans. I had paid for my school through running, and Jeremy had worked to pay for his. Neither of us had credit card debt. I had never even had a credit card, and Jeremy had paid cash for his antique car collection.

When it came to saving, we discovered that I was the saver and Jer was the spender in our relationship. My dad is a financial adviser who has owned his own asset management company for nearly two decades, so I grew up learning the basic principles of investing—not to mention I went to business school. Jer, on the other hand, was trained to buy projects that would one day turn into investments.

When we discussed giving, Jeremy and I confessed that we periodically tithed a portion of the little we made to the church and tried to help our friends in need when we could. Chris and Jamie stretched us here. They asked us to think of ways we could be more intentional about giving generously (Deuteronomy 15:10). Jeremy expressed his heart for the homeless, and I expressed my heart for high schoolers and the ministry of Young Life. This helped us develop a framework for consistent giving during our first year of marriage. We were encouraged to cultivate a spirit of generosity at the beginning of our marriage rather than waiting to establish giving habits later on.

As we talked about budgeting and spending, we laid out our financial goals and talked about what to do in times of both scarcity and abundance. We identified what we valued and wanted to spend money on so we could make a budget and save for things such as holidays, gifts, vacations, eating out, new clothes, and other discretionary expenses.

In our conversation about sex, the Herbs encouraged us to share our past mistakes with one another and to ask for forgiveness. This was part of "the Illumination of the Past" so nothing would cloud our ability to imagine the future.[1] We also made a plan and set some boundaries for pursuing purity until and then beyond our wedding day.

Then we talked about "the first time." You may think that talking with our counselors about the night we were going to lose our virginity would be unfathomably awkward, but it was actually quite helpful. It prompted us to have honest conversations that we would likely otherwise have avoided. Chris and Jamie gave us a reality check when it came to sex. Jer and I had envisioned sex to be a natural, pleasurable thing that we both would intuitively know exactly how to do. They set our expectations straight and told us not to be discouraged by the inevitable learning curve. They suggested taking one of two different approaches to sex in the beginning. The first was just doing it and learning as we went, and the second was literally talking through it and learning each other's preferences. This was a valuable piece of advice that we took into our honeymoon. It helped us get past the things we might otherwise have been afraid to ask each other or be honest about.

Chris and Jamie also freed us from the pressure that Christian culture puts on having sex for the first time after the longest day of your life—your wedding day. It was comforting to know that we weren't failures if indeed we were just too tired, although that definitely did not end up being the case. Did I mention that we burned with passion? We probably would have gotten a speeding ticket for rushing to our hotel, but since our getaway car was Rain—Jer's 1976 Land Cruiser, which was covered in hops and trailing wedding cans—it kept the suspense building as we watched the honking cars breeze past us in the fast lane.

After each session, Chris and Jamie gave us assignments to complete before the next session. For example, after the first session, they asked us to journal and reflect on that session and come back with some thoughts and questions. Another assignment was to write down our expectations for each other as spiritual partners. Perhaps the most interesting assignment was to talk to our parents or grandparents about "generational sin," which was something we'd never heard of. Jer will talk about this in a moment. This took our "illumination of the past" to a whole new level. Every session, assignment, and question were opportunities to learn more about marriage, each other, and ourselves as a couple.

On the car rides home from our sessions at the Herbs's house (which was in Corvallis, about 90 minutes from our parents' houses), we often felt overwhelmed by the emotional heaviness of what we discussed and by the sheer volume of new information we had to absorb. Premarital counseling exposed old wounds, bad habits, and unhealthy relational patterns. I know this sounds like a ton of work, but we knew it would have a lifelong payoff.

The reality is that most people in our generation are willing to work way harder to plan their perfect wedding day than they are to prepare for the promise. And as hard as planning a wedding can be, preparing for marriage is harder because it requires exposing the more vulnerable areas of our lives. I think this is why the majority of our generation skip out on premarital counseling—they're afraid of being vulnerable, exposing their struggles, and receiving hard truth.

If you are engaged and still haven't had any hard conversations, shared any secret struggles, or shed any tears, you're well past demo day. Bringing the hard and hurtful stuff into the light in the beginning will help to protect you from a hard and hurtful ending. It's not for the faint of heart. It's trying, time-consuming, and often tearful, but if you don't illuminate the dark past, it will be much harder to imagine a bright future.

JEREMY

When Chris and Jamie raised the issue of generational sin, Audrey and I looked at them with our heads tilted and eyebrows raised. *What's that?* They explained that sin and dysfunction can be passed on from one generation to the next. It's what happens when destructive habits and patterns—such as dishonesty, addiction, infidelity, divorce, domestic violence, racism, financial irresponsibility, and the like—persist in successive generations of a family. I think most of us would like to believe we are simply the person we have chosen to become, but the truth is more complex than that. We are also by-products of our parents—the good things about them as well as the not-so-good things.

Just to be clear, you are not your parents. If your parents are a wreck, that doesn't mean you will be. It just means there are patterns of thought and behavior from your upbringing that may be hardwired into you. And if you aren't aware of these patterns, you'll not only repeat them in your own life, but you'll also bring them into marriage and eventually pass them along to your children. Audrey and I were about to merge our two families and become a new family, and we were inevitably going to be dragging along with us things that need improvement.

My grandparents, Papa and Honey, have a binder of the Roloff family tree that traces our genealogy as far back as they could discover. Before our wedding I sat down with them, and we talked for a few hours about the good and the not-so-good traits in the Roloff family tree.

Knowing where my family had been prone to dysfunction, failure, and sin was enlightening. It wasn't anything to be fixed overnight, of course, but rather it was information to call to mind in the event that after we've been married for twenty years and some of these things start showing up, we know why and can address them with reason and understanding. It also gave us something specific to pray against in the present, with the hope of saving us years of confusion, addiction, and hurt. Sometimes all it takes to prevent something is simply knowing about it and praying against it.

The Herbs also helped us take a closer look at our own upbringing. As a boy, I had immense freedom, and I loved it! Part of this was because I grew up on a large farm, but it was also just my folks' parenting style. There were nights when I literally did not come home. I'd be out camping somewhere on the farm or sleeping in cowboy town. My mom demanded that I let her know when I did that, and I did, but even so, I had the freedom to do it. It had never occurred to me that my childhood experiences of freedom had the potential to affect how I acted in my marriage.

Once again, Audrey's experience was very different from mine. She was raised in a fairly strict, orderly household. Her family tree is full of collegiate athletes, professional musicians, and career achievers—in other words, people who lived with discipline and rigid schedules. There was nothing better or worse about the ways we were raised, but we were definitely glad to know about the differences!

As the big day drew closer, our differences started emerging more and more. Your wedding will likely be the first big thing you plan with your significant other. There will be stress, to-do lists, budgeting, and a timeline. Knowing how Audrey was raised was helpful during our first big event together, because, Lord willing, I wanted there to be many more—having kids, buying a house, pursuing careers, and so on. How we handle money, act under stress, and make decisions are all tied up in our upbringing and our beliefs about the world.

In an effort to protect my family, since many of you know who they are, I won't share details about what I talked about with my grandparents pertaining to generational sin. However, I have a friend from college who has an insightful story about how he illuminated his past, recognized areas of dysfunction, and changed his future.

One night, I was hanging with Joe and his wife at The Lark in Santa Barbara. They had been married for six years and had just moved out of her parents' house. Curious about their story, I began to ask questions, and in no time at all, Joe had me wrapped up in their story.

Immediately after getting married, Joe and his wife, Tammy, began having financial problems. After two years of financial distress, they had to move in with her parents. In his search for answers, Joe discovered the work of author and financial adviser Dave Ramsey and began to analyze how he and his wife were spending their money. After working through Ramsey's process, he realized that their approach to money was underdeveloped and haphazard, partly because of how he was raised to think about money. He vowed to recalibrate his life in this area.

Through two and a half years of discipline and sacrifice, he and Tammy have paid off $30,000 of debt, bought a house, created a retirement plan, started a college fund for their two boys, and become faithful in monthly tithing. They are on schedule to pay off their house before they reach the age of forty. Did I mention that Joe dropped out of college, has a promising career ahead of him, and his wife is now a stay-at-home mom?

After some self-reflection and hard work, he is changing the generational patterns that have to do with money in his family. And he's helping others do the same. Through his transparency about his own struggles, he helped me realize that I had lots to learn in this area as I was planning and preparing to provide for a family of my own.

I love Joe's story because it's a perfect example of what it means to break the generational cycle of dysfunction. He noticed that things could be better, identified his own struggles, reflected on his thoughts and behaviors, and decided to become the person he needed to be to change his family tree for the better.

*　*　*

Once we get to the "preparing for the promise" phase, we should know the basics. *Do we share the same love of Christ and value of the Word of God? What is our vision for family? Do we want to have children? Where do we desire to live? What are our career goals? Does or will our job require large amounts of travel?* These are all conversations to have when considering marriage. I love how Pastor John Mark Comer put it in his book *Loveology*:

> Don't get married because you think he or she is "the one." Trust me, they're not. There's no such thing! But *do* get married when you see who God is making somebody to be, and it lights you up. When you want to be a part of that story of transformation. That journey to the future. When you are well aware it will be a long and bumpy ride, but you don't want to miss one mile. Because you believe in God's calling on them, and you want in.[2]

Once you've discerned this to be true of the person you are dating, you can begin the strenuous but strengthening process of "the illumination of the past." Illuminating the past is a challenge, but it's also one of the most helpful things Audrey and I did to prepare for our marriage. Without it, we wouldn't have been able to create a clear vision and mission for our future.

AUDREY

In some ways, the process of illumination is a lot like chess. Sometimes you have to move backward before you can move forward, and sometimes you have to sacrifice pieces in order to set yourself up for the next few moves. Illuminating the past (moving backward) helped us develop a strategy, a playbook of sorts, for imagining our future (moving forward). It helped us cultivate a vision for our family, refine our mission as a married couple, and discern our dreams and desires.

We dreamed of traveling for a season—camping, road tripping, and living minimally. We dreamed of one day starting a ministry together and combining our individual gifts and skills to inspire, encourage, and transform lives. We asked each other questions about when to start a family, how we wanted to live, who we wanted to surround ourselves with, and what we wanted to be known for. We talked about our hopes of one day raising our own family on our own land—whether that meant continuing the legacy on Roloff Farms or building our own—and we were unified in this vision.

We had talked casually about some of these things when we were dating, but I'm thankful we waited until we were engaged to wade more deeply into these topics. I think talking about generational sin, sex, and our darkest secrets too early in our dating relationship might have created a lot of unnecessary pressure. Christians especially can get a little carried away with this. We think we need to know if he or she is "the one" on our first date. No, please just stop. Relax a little and enjoy just getting to know this person!

You don't need to cross-examine a first date with questions about every aspect and ambition of his or her life. And to add to that point, there is no such thing as "the one." I know, how unromantic of me to say, but really, let this idea go. It is in no way biblical, and it does us more harm than good when it comes to dating, love, and marriage. There are probably many people out there with whom you could write a beautiful love story and end up marrying. However, the moment I said "I do" on our wedding day, Jeremy became "the one," till death do us part.

I think we need to start approaching dating much more like we approach new friendships. Not kindergarten friendships, but adult friendships. Kindergarten friendships develop a lot like one-night stands. You meet, and you're instantly ready to have sleepovers. But healthy adult friendships are marked by intentionality, trust, and camaraderie. Dating, much like developing a new friendship, offers the freedom to get to know someone without the commitment of forever. It doesn't mean sharing every intricate detail of your life story on coffee date number one, but it doesn't mean dating for two years and never sharing your struggles either.

* * *

Once you're engaged, it's time to fully unveil your struggles, sins, and secrets. It's time to bring your darkness to the light. It's time to illuminate the past so you can clearly see who you are marrying. Too many relationships never get to the "fully known and fully loved" stage because they are hobbled by fear or pride. She's afraid he won't love her if she tells him about her borderline eating disorder. She's too prideful to talk about her dysfunctional childhood. She's afraid he won't love her if he knows about her anxiety. Or he's too prideful to admit his porn addiction. He's afraid she won't love him if she knew how his parents' marriage failed. He's too prideful to confess his drinking habits. Fill in the blank with your own issues.

Through our premarital counseling we learned the importance of leaving nothing in the dark with each other. We committed to a windows-open, no-secrets policy that has promoted integrity and healthy communication in our marriage. I'll be honest, the journey to "I do" was hard, heavy, and humbling. Walking in darkness is a faulty defense mechanism; it always ends up piercing the heart it aimed to protect.

Momentary honesty may sting, but long-term lies are infectious. Don't fall prey to infection's darkness. Choose to bring everything to the light—with each other, with the Lord, and with others—so you can embrace the freedom that honesty offers. Light always prevails against darkness. Illuminating the dark past and imagining the bright future helped us lay a solid foundation for our first year of marriage and beyond. We were determined to protect our love on the road to oneness.

9

OUR CODE OF
Conflict

AUDREY

Our wedding day was just a couple months away, and I was so ready to have some alone time with Jeremy. Finally no film crew, no meetings with landlords, no wedding vendors, no premarital counseling, and no bachelor parties or bridal showers. Jeremy was coming home from school for a week. The days filled up quickly with to-dos, but we intentionally set aside one day to simply spend time together. Time to play, laugh, and not take ourselves so seriously.

We had planned to have dinner the night Jeremy flew back into town, but thanks to the always-delayed flights at the San Francisco airport, his flight became an unintentional red-eye. We had to cancel our dinner plans, but Jeremy texted me late that night and said he'd be at my house first thing in the morning, promising we would spend the day together. He rumbled up to my house in Rain before sunrise, with a full thermos of coffee and a day-date mission all planned out. I raced out to the street to meet him before he could come to the door. After a long "I've missed you" embrace, he smiled at me and said, "Let's go to the coast for the day."

In true Oregonian fashion, we stopped at the iconic Camp 18 Restaurant for brunch. Camp 18 is a Bunyanesque log cabin nestled in the woods at mile marker 18 along the winding coastal highway. The cabin is surrounded by logging artifacts from the 1970s, making the property a historic playground of antiques. Of course, Jer and I are suckers for anything with an ounce of nostalgia, so we always loved stopping for brunch, wandering around the vintage train cars, and climbing up the old water tower before driving the rest of the way to the beach.

On the way there, we talked about a few scheduling things. Jer briefed me on when we were filming that week, and I downloaded him on wedding vendors we still needed to book. We didn't get too deep into conversation because it's always a little hard to talk in Rain. The road noise is epic.

After rummaging through the old artifacts and taking a few photos, we headed into the restaurant for some lumberjack pancakes and colossal cinnamon rolls—our kind of wedding diet food. While we waited for our meal, I was expecting to have some stimulating conversation about what we had been learning lately, which beaches we would explore, or what we might do on our honeymoon, but instead I ended up feeling like I was dining alone.

Jer hardly looked at me and wouldn't engage in conversation. He kept looking around the restaurant, and every now and then, he'd say things like, "I wonder how they got that beam to run across the whole ceiling like that." I glared back at him with an "are you kidding me?" look on my face. If you had been seated at the table next to us, you might have thought we were on the world's worst first date. I grew more enraged as time went on and started to express my frustration through cutting remarks. In an effort to evoke some kind of an emotional response, I said, "Maybe we should just head back after lunch. I'm tired." But he wasn't fazed.

"Really? Okay, we can do that if you want," he replied stoically.

Where did I go wrong in this conversation? Why are we acting like we hate each other? Our lack of connection made me feel confused, afflicted, and self-conscious. I tried to patiently wait for him to come back to earth and act like I existed, but when we got our food and continued to eat in silence, my emotions got the best of me. When we finished eating, I stood up and told Jer I'd wait for him outside while he waited for the bill.

A few minutes later, Jeremy came out, and we walked to Rain in silence. What was supposed to be a fun day of playing and laughing together was quickly turning into a fight. Disheartened that our day was ruined, I sunk into the passenger seat, feeling torn between anger and sadness, between the desire to prove my point and the desire to reconcile.

Terri Clark sings a country song that sums up how I feel sometimes when Jeremy and I fight.[1] There's a line that goes, "I just wanna be mad for a while." To this day, Jer tries to "make me smile," to defuse our conflict with humor, but sometimes I just wanna be mad for a while. This was definitely one of those times.

We got in the car, and Jer made a joke about a guy leaving the restaurant who clearly looked like he'd been living on Camp 18 cinnamon rolls. Instead of laughing, I clenched my teeth, kept a scowl on my face, and avoided eye contact. I felt like he was trying to antagonize me by proving that he didn't notice or care that I was clearly upset.

As he fired up the engine in Rain, he said, "So, you still wanna go to the beach or you wanna head back?" His question broke me. With blurry eyes I finally looked at him and vented my frustrations. "Can you please help me understand why you're treating me like I don't exist?"

This prompted a long conversation about expectations and communication. We talked in circles about it on and off for the rest of the drive out to the coast. One thing became clear: our conflict was rooted in poorly communicated expectations.

If you've been in a relationship for any length of time, you have probably experienced a similar situation. You know, those moments when what *actually* happened was different than what was *supposed to* happen. When you were supposed to engage in stimulating and soul-stirring conversation over brunch, but instead your fiancé spent the entire time analyzing the structural integrity of the restaurant and acting like he wanted nothing to do with you. Cool.

I just assumed Jeremy understood that I would want to jump right into talking about everything going on in our lives since we'd last seen each other, but that wasn't the case. Everything I was so eager to talk about felt stressful and heavy to Jeremy. He just needed some time to adjust to being back together before diving into the black hole of decision making and deep conversations. Where I felt like the healthiest thing for our relationship was to communicate about everything, Jer felt like the healthiest thing was to just exist together and simply *be* for a while. We had become so focused on apartment hunting, job searching, wedding planning, and marriage stuff that it had been a long time since we enjoyed doing something together without an agenda. Unknown to me, Jeremy craved that. Unknown to Jeremy, I craved quality *communication*, not just quality *time*.

This is what the test says about people like me whose primary love language is Quality Time: "Distractions, postponed dates, or the failure to listen can be especially hurtful. Quality Time also means sharing quality conversation and quality activities."[2] Because the majority of our dating relationship was long-distance, it was hard to spend quality time together. Whenever we had the opportunity to be together, I placed a high value on quality conversation and activities. When our Camp 18 date was completely devoid of quality conversation, I felt hurt and frustrated. I felt *un*loved; therefore, I reacted poorly.

Through all of this, we realized that if one of us is expecting to get something out of a situation that the other person has no idea they are supposed to give, the disappointment of unmet expectations is the inevitable outcome. So we talked about a few ways we could prevent the breakfast date debacle from reoccurring, one of which was clearly communicating our expectations.

For us, communicating expectations often begins with a quick check-in while we're in the car on the way to an event or lying in bed the night before a big day. It's as easy as asking, "What are your expectations for this party [gathering, event, day, vacation, etc.]?" Yes, it really is this simple. This question helps us clearly understand each other's wants, hopes, and needs, and it gets us on the same page. It helps facilitate unity, connection, satisfaction, and win-win situations. It helps us avoid potential conflicts because we know ahead of time that one of us wants to leave early or spend time with his or her parents or maybe do different things afterward. You get the idea.

We've found this to be so helpful in our marriage. Even so, we're far from having perfected the art of expectation management. Like everything in life, learning to communicate our expectations demands practice. We still occasionally fail to communicate our expectations well, and we still react poorly when one of us disappoints the other. But we are on a pilgrimage of learning how to love each other well, which makes every conflict an opportunity to learn more about how we can prevent conflict in the future.

In addition to communicating expectations in advance, our Camp 18 date gone awry also helped us discover one more simple strategy for avoiding conflict—physical touch. You'll remember from a few chapters back that Jer is a Nine on the Enneagram and that one of his love languages is Physical Touch. Well, one tendency of a Nine is to become so distracted by or preoccupied with their surroundings that they get lost in their thoughts and appear to be completely detached from personal interaction. That's what I experienced at Camp 18 while I was sitting at the table patiently waiting for him to come back to earth. But we discovered that if I simply reach over and touch Jer's shoulder or arm when he's preoccupied, it helps him reconnect and be present in the conversation. So whenever I feel like Jer's not listening or his brain is on a rocket ship far away from our conversation, I will reach over and put my hand on his arm.

I can't be the only one who has experienced this. Maybe in your current relationship, you've found yourself saying things like this:

- Are you even listening to me?
- Did you hear what I just said?
- How many times do I have to say it?
- Do you realize this is the fifth time I've told you?
- Don't make me say it again.

Instead of sounding like a nagging broken record and becoming increasingly frustrated with Jeremy, I've learned to simply reach over and put my hand on his shoulder when he's working on something and I have something to ask or say—especially if he's preoccupied with something else at the time. I can't tell you how many times I've asked Jer before leaving our house, "Do you have your wallet?" and he immediately responds, "Yeah, I got it!" But when we arrive at our destination, he says, "Oh shoot, babe, I forgot my wallet!" You can imagine my frustration. This scenario has often escalated into a dispute. So now, I just touch Jeremy when I need to remind him about something or ask a question, or if it's clear he's simply lost in thought. This doesn't mean Jeremy has a free pass to just check out until I touch him. He is also learning to break the habit of routinely responding to me without *really* hearing what I'm saying.

Our willingness to learn from our conflicts has become one of our best strategies for keeping them from reoccurring. Without this willingness, we wouldn't have discovered the importance of communicating our expectations and of physical touch for keeping us on the same page in conversations. These solutions have become massive marching steps forward on our road to oneness.

JEREMY

Unlike our Camp 18 fight, which was quickly and easily resolved, there was another conflict that required a lot more time and effort to untangle.

After Audrey and I had broken up, I experienced an unexpected freedom—the freedom to be fully present where I was. I was no longer living with my body in Santa Barbara and my mind in Corvallis with Audrey. Even though I had the strong hope we'd get back together, it was a relief to be able to enjoy college and be fully invested—mind and body—in Santa Barbara.

While we were together, I had been intentional about protecting our love by being cautious about who I spent time with, but now I felt free to hang out with many more people than I had been before. Volunteering at church, I met a lot of great people and got plugged into a small group of college students I started hanging out with all the time.

I had taken Blue Moon with me to school, and it became the vehicle of choice among my friends—and the women seemed to like it too. We would cruise to the beach or simply drive around town enjoying the looks Blue Moon got and the atmosphere that came with hanging out in a vintage VW bus. We made many trips up to the Lizard's Mouth trail for afternoon hikes, and one time we camped among the rocks and watched the city below twinkle like stars above the dark sea. Having a crew to hang out with made Santa Barbara feel like home, and I could tell that my friends enjoyed having me—all of me—there with them.

There was a girl in our crew whom I started to develop a unique friendship with. Kate and I started spending a lot of time together, picking each other up from work and school to go for drives in the Santa Ynez Mountains, meeting up with friends for iced coffee and people watching, or carpooling to worship nights and hangouts.

Kate was very connected in the Santa Barbara community and knew the city well. I was thankful to have a friend who introduced me to so many other friends and showed me around Santa Barbara. We laughed an awful lot and enjoyed being together. Our mutual friends thought of us as having a brother-sister relationship. Although I never considered her more than a friend, we became emotionally close. I was enjoying spending all this time with my friends in Santa Barbara and focusing on my new relationships, but Audrey was always at the back of my mind.

That summer, my roommate Tye joined me on a trip home to Portland. This was the visit when I showed up unannounced at Audrey's twenty-first birthday party. And you already know what happened next—before the weekend was done, we had confessed our mutual longing to be with each other again, despite the challenges, and had recommitted to dating.

Then I returned to my life in Santa Barbara and rejoined my friends. At this point, Kate had become one of my best friends and was excited to hear the news. Because it was a platonic relationship and Audrey knew all about it, it never occurred to me that my friendship with Kate would have to change as my relationship with Audrey grew. However, during our breakup, I had confided in Kate, which made us emotionally close.

Once Auj and I were dating again, our relationship began to deepen and progress. Now that the pressure was off and we were treating our long-distance relationship with appropriate expectations, we only desired each other more. Our love grew, and it wasn't long until we were discussing marriage. As Sheldon Vanauken writes, "For love must grow or die."[3] This is when my relationship with Kate started to become a problem.

I came home for winter break, and Audrey and I spent every moment together. After a couple of weeks full of snow missions, tree lightings, and Christmas traditions, we headed back to school, and long distance became more grueling. Audrey and I missed each other fiercely, and we hated not being able to do life together. We longed to do the simplest things together, like homework, grocery shopping, and watching movies, but we couldn't. When I went back to Santa Barbara, Audrey saw, through social media, that I was doing these things with Kate. This led to our first conversation about how my relationship with Kate needed to change.

Auj kindly asked me to stop hanging out alone with Kate as much as I had been. A justifiable thing to ask and something I should have listened to, but I didn't. I was quick to write it off. "Auj, my relationship with Kate is 100 percent friendship. I am madly in love with you, and I choose you—always."

In my relationship ignorance, I tried to rationalize my closeness with Kate. *How could I pull back from a close friend, a sister in Christ?* And from there, I began to mess everything up. I sidestepped talking to Kate and Auj about it because I wanted to avoid the whole conflict, but the longer I put it off, the worse it got. I assured Auj that we had stopped hanging out alone, but it was a difficult situation because we had all the same friends. Regardless, I agreed to make an effort to avoid any situation that could lead to hanging out alone.

Kate started asking me when she could come up and visit the farm because it was something I was always talking about and she hadn't seen it yet. And let's be real, who wouldn't want to visit the farm? I always loved showing people the farm for the first time, but I was reluctant to invite Kate because I wanted to spend every minute of my time at home with Audrey.

However, Kate flew out to surprise me in the springtime when I was home visiting Audrey on my break from school. Audrey held her tongue and tried to be a trouper during Kate's visit, but as soon as Kate left, Audrey vented her frustrations and emotions.

I had messed up. I should have been honest with Kate and told her I needed to take a step back in our relationship in order to grow in my relationship with Audrey, but I didn't. I avoided a hard conversation with Kate in an effort to keep the peace, but my efforts had the reverse effect. I created conflict and ended up hurting both Kate and Audrey.

The situation wasn't looking good. Audrey was beginning to question my loyalty. "I'm the one you're marrying, not her," she said. I understood where Audrey was coming from—I couldn't imagine what it would do to me if she became best friends—better friends—with another dude. And yet that's exactly what I was doing to her! The kind of inside joking and camaraderie that Kate and I shared was difficult for Audrey and me to experience because Audrey was a thousand miles away and we only got to see each other every few months.

I felt horrible about the whole situation. But when I told Audrey that I also cared about Kate's feelings, her reply put me in check. "You're afraid of hurting her feelings? What about my feelings? I'm hurt, confused, and frankly surprised. Why are you unwilling to sacrifice your friendship for our love?"

Now I was in a mess because I had never talked to Kate about how our friendship needed to change once I started dating Audrey again. People-pleaser problems. Weeks of inner turmoil and confusion followed. I was navigating uncharted waters that eventually left the whole situation shipwrecked, but through it all I learned several hard lessons.

I eventually sought counsel from close friends and a mentor, all of whom were married. I had resisted doing so up to this point, perhaps because I didn't want to hear what I guessed they might say. Each person advised me to loosen my grip. "This friendship is incompatible with marriage," they said. I understood why, but I had trouble dealing with it, mostly because I had trouble dealing with conflict. I came to learn this about myself from our premarital counseling sessions (and from studying the Enneagram), but now Audrey and I were experiencing the repercussions in a dramatic way.

Believe it or not, it wasn't until right before our wedding that

I finally understood the weight and ramifications of my choices. When it hit me that my inability to let go of Kate meant Audrey and I were continually being separated in spirit and closeness, I broke down. We later referred to this day as "The Breakdown."

I realized that I was, and to some degree still am, an underground people pleaser. I say "underground" because I'm not a people pleaser in the obvious, pushover sense of the term, but rather in the sense that I aim to escape conflict through people pleasing. My deepest desire was to be one with Auj, but my strongest desire was to make everyone happy without having to sacrifice anything.

I didn't assume that Audrey would just forgive me right away, so I was nervous to ask for her forgiveness, but I did anyway. "I hate that I've hurt you through this, Auj. Will you forgive me?" I sincerely apologized to Audrey, and we held each other in a heap of tears and consolation. This was the first time Auj had seen me cry. Remember, my emotional wall was refusing to show emotion or escaping it. Well, this was demo day for that wall.

I promised Audrey that the wedding would mark the end of my friendship with Kate. It had come to that point. It wasn't a friendship I could healthily maintain. I had been wrong to try. I finally understood how continuing to pursue my friendship with Kate was infringing on my oneness with Audrey and stomping all over her heart in the process.

Audrey's desire to reconcile and move on was greater than her desire to prove a point. "Yes, babe, I love you. Can we just put this past us for good?" Through tears, I looked at Audrey and assured her that no one would ever come between us like this again. We exchanged "I love you"s and spent some time together that evening—just the two of us. Life-giving and laughter-filled conversations around the campfire were just what our spirits needed.

A lesson learned the hard way is better than one not learned at all. My friendship with Kate was initially a good one—a great one—but there came a time when it started taking away from my relationship with Audrey. Audrey wanted to be my best friend, and I wanted to be Audrey's best friend, but my actions were communicating something else. And actions speak louder than words. My inability to loosen my grip on my friendship with Kate was effectively telling Audrey that Kate had my loyalty—that I was more afraid of hurting her than I was of hurting Audrey.

There's nothing wrong with having close friendships while single and dating. However, as marriage approaches and you gain ground on the road to oneness, relationships you have with those of the opposite sex may need to change. If oneness is your goal, which it should be, then it should start to feel weird, maybe even a little dangerous, to have a very close friend of the opposite sex—for example, having a friend with whom you routinely meet up alone for lunch or coffee, which turns into things such as venting about life, connecting emotionally, texting after hours, and so forth. Even in our innocence—or perhaps it's better to call it ignorance—such friendships are bound to create conflict with our beloved.

It took longer than it should have for me to understand why Audrey was hurt. I insisted that my relationship with Kate was harmless while Audrey was expressing serious hurt. I know, it doesn't make sense. Investing emotionally in an opposite-sex friendship that leads to soulful exploration is dangerous. These kinds of relationships can be breeding grounds for an emotional affair.

According to the American Association of Marriage and Family Therapy, about 35 percent of wives and 45 percent of husbands report having emotional affairs.[4] An emotional affair is essentially a bond between two people that resembles the closeness and emotional intimacy of a romantic relationship while never being physically intimate.

Don't misinterpret me. I'm not saying you can't have friends or coworkers of the opposite sex. I have many female friends. However, I have boundaries to protect my union with Audrey. I trust her, and she trusts me, but it takes more than trust to protect something. The statistics don't lie. Emotional affairs are common and can be dangerous. Most emotional affairs started out with two friends, innocent intentions, and a marriage that didn't use boundaries to protect its union.

To experience the heights of love, we must live into what the Bible says marriage should be—complete oneness. In my situation, conflict arose when I resisted the sacrifice needed to pursue oneness. I tell you this story because I think that—unfortunately—most people in relationships will be able to relate to it at some point. I had to swallow my pride and be willing to sacrifice certain freedoms, such as the freedom to be close friends with whomever I wanted. Initially, I was resistant because ending my friendship with Kate was difficult—sacrifice always is. But sacrifice for the strength of a greater union—your marriage—will always be worth it.

Most couples probably have parts of their love story they wish they could rewrite, and this is one of ours. By sharing my story, I hope to help you make better choices than I did. Had I been up front with Kate in the beginning, I could have protected both Audrey and Kate from hurt and frustration. All I can do is learn from it and share what I learned in hopes of preventing others from having to endure the same painful ramifications. As much as I wish I could change what happened, I trust that God wanted us to learn the dangers of emotionally intimate opposite-sex friendships *before* we were married, and for that I am thankful.

* * *

Don't let *The Notebook*'s famous line fool you. Nobody should ever say, "Well, that's what we do! We fight!"[5] Conflict is inevitable in relationships, but fighting is preventable. We learned a lot from our Camp 18 fight and my emotionally intimate friendship with Kate—mostly how not to handle conflict—but it also got us thinking about some boundaries we could set to prevent future conflict. The health of our marriage would be determined not by an absence of conflict, but rather by our ability to handle conflict well. So we asked each other a few questions that helped us set our "code of conflict":

- What steps can we take to prevent tension from evolving into turmoil?
- What parameters or boundaries can we set so that our fighting is healthy and productive rather than harmful and destructive?
- If we're going to fight, how do we fight fair?
- What can we do to speed the process of repentance, forgiveness, and reconciliation so that we don't linger in hurt and dysfunction?

We agreed it was a good idea to work through these questions before we said "I do." So we sought guidance from the Word of God and from our premarital counselors. The result was our code of conflict—rules aimed at preventing conflict, handling conflict, and promoting quick resolution. Some of these rules were inspired by couples who were farther along in their marriage journey, and some we learned from our own fights and failures:

- Don't fight in public.
- Remind each other you're on the same team when disagreements arise.
- Hold hands while resolving conflict.
- Ask the "what are your expectations for this?" question.
- Eliminate *never* and *always* from your statements about each other.
- Have cooling-off periods.
- Always say, "I forgive you."
- Don't vent conflict to other people, unless it's to a mentor or in an effort to resolve the issue.
- Pray about it more than you talk about it.
- Resist trying to resolve conflict over the phone.
- Don't withhold sex to prove a point or position yourself.
- When angry, don't sleep in separate beds, on the couch, or at a friend's house.
- Pursue a resolution over a compromise.

Have you discussed a code for conflict for your relationship? In our marriage, we use it as a way to keep the playing field fair and square, and the more we use it, the less fouls we commit. This has helped prevent arguments from turning into fights. It has reminded us that we are on the same team. It has encouraged us to respond rather than react. It has provided detours away from situations that may have otherwise escalated into hurtful words and disrespectful actions. It has urged us to be givers and forgivers. And it has protected our oneness.

10

THE ROAD TO
Oneness

JEREMY

Holding hands as we approached the big glass door, I skipped a step ahead to open it for Audrey. "Here we go," I whispered as it swung open. Once we stepped inside the Volkswagen dealership, it wasn't five seconds before a gentleman with a cheeky grin walked up and reached out his hand.

"Good afternoon!" said the eager car salesman. "What can I do for you today?"

"We'd like to look at your 2012 Jetta TDI SportWagen," I replied.

"Yes, of course!" he said. "Right this way. Would you like a cup of coffee?"

It was seven days before our wedding, and we needed to buy a car. Audrey had accepted a job in Los Angeles selling wine, and we needed a car big enough for her to transport cargo. Our move date was set for two days after returning from our honeymoon, so we'd have no time to car shop after the wedding.

We had a preferred car in mind, but we decided to also check out a used TDI SportWagen as we'd heard good things about it, and the price was more in line with our budget. The gas mileage situation was also favorable, which was a significant plus, given that we'd soon be braving LA traffic on a daily basis. On our test-drive, Audrey and I glanced at each other and exchanged discreet grins, being cautious not to show too much enthusiasm in front of the sales guy. We loved how roomy it was, how smoothly it drove, and how it had a huge sunroof to let the California sunshine pour in. Plus, Auj fancied a white car.

We liked the car way more than we had expected, but we tried to play it cool. Pulling back into the dealership after the test-drive, the salesman, who seemed to be a genuinely nice guy, asked us how we liked it.

"It's nice," I replied. I had heard that showing too much interest to a used car salesman is bad negotiating, so I tried my best to appear ambivalent. "There are a few cars across the street at the Subaru dealership that we want to check out," I said. "We'll be back later if we're interested."

We hurried across the street to the other dealership in excitement. Rounding the corner, there she was—a brand-new Subaru Outback. Walking into the showroom, we embarked on the same routine. Handshake, big grin, coffee, small talk while walking to the car, test-drive, and then the big question, "Well, what do you think?"

We loved it, but it was also outside of our budget and we felt a little uncomfortable starting out our marriage with an expensive new car. I was also feeling a little uncertain about the process.

Although I had a lot of experience with Craigslist purchases, neither of us had ever bought a car from a dealership before, and everything felt like a scam.

After pacing the sidewalk outside and making a few phone calls, Audrey and I looked at each other with tired eyes. "We have enough decisions to make," I finally said. "Let's just go for it." Walking back into the dealership, I gave the Subaru guy a thumbs-up. Everybody was excited, and we refilled our coffee cups on the way back to the tiny cubicle where it all goes down. After about an hour of helping us choose the model and discussing our loan, the sales guy got up and said he'd be back in a bit with the final paperwork for signatures. "Sounds like a plan," I said, leaning back in my chair.

A few minutes went by, and Audrey put her hand on my leg—the leg I had been unconsciously bouncing up and down. "What are you thinking about?" she asked.

"I still have a funny feeling," I admitted. "I kinda liked that other car."

"Me too!" she said, excited that we were thinking the same thing.

"Really?" I said. "Dang, we're in too deep now though. I think this one will still be good."

I was trying to convince myself and Auj, but it was obvious we were both uncertain. Then the sales guy came back and said he was having some technical difficulty with the printer but that it shouldn't be much longer. Another thirty minutes passed, and the uneasy feeling in my gut began to grow. I looked up at the clock and realized we had only another forty-five minutes before the VW dealership across the street closed.

"Babe," I said, "let's go get that other car."

Audrey looked at me with big eyes and an even bigger grin. "But what do we say?" she asked. "How do we leave?"

I grabbed her hand, smiled back, and said, "Let's just leave."

We felt like bandits as we stood and then tiptoed to the front door. Just as my hand touched the door, we heard a woman's voice behind us say, "Can I help you with anything?"

Turning around, I paused for a moment and then said, "No, we're fine, but we have to go. Can you tell him we don't want the car?" I didn't want to be rude, but you know how it is with salespeople. They don't take no for an answer. And we were running out of time. The woman looked confused, but before she could try to convince us to stay, we bolted out the door and burst out laughing.

We ran across the parking lot and headed back across the street for the used, more affordable VW wagon just as the dealership was about to close. This felt right. We wondered if maybe that technical difficulty with the printer was the Lord protecting us from a regrettable decision. Holding hands, we déjà vu-ed back through the big glass door at the VW dealer as Audrey looked up at me and said, "Good call, babe."

Following our gut, we were unified in our decision and it felt right.

Our grinning salesman was both surprised and happy to see us. "We'll take her!" I said.

Grabbing yet another cup of coffee, because Folgers will always have a special place in my heart, we headed for the cubicle, this time with a peaceful spirit. It was nearly 10 p.m. at this point, and the dealership was almost ready to close, but the salesman assured us it wouldn't be a problem. When the process took longer than expected, we ordered pizza for everyone who stayed after hours to help us finish up. It was 12:45 a.m. by the time we finally drove off the lot in our new-to-us car. It was a fun first-car buying experience and a successful mission on our road to oneness.

This would be Audrey's car, but we agreed to call it *our* car. If we were soon to become one in flesh and spirit, then we decided to also become one with our pronouns and possessions. Nothing destroys oneness as quickly as self-centeredness, and the subtleties of self-centeredness begin with our speech. Embracing the principle of sharing to guard against the language of self, we named our new-to-us car The Wagon in an effort to become us-centered, not self-centered. So instead of always saying "Audrey's car," we just called it "The Wagon." It became an "us thing" instead of a "her [or me] thing." The fact that I had already named all of my rigs helped this as well. The principle of oneness infiltrates all areas of our life—our language, our body, our possessions, and even our finances.

We had joined our bank accounts a week prior in order to buy *our* car with what would soon become *our* money. If we were going to be sharing a bed, an apartment, a car, and a last name, why wouldn't we share our finances? Oneness is the reality of what God has already proclaimed about marriage. If we truly are "one flesh" with our spouse, then it stands to reason that there are no off-limits when it comes to pursuing this oneness.

AUDREY

In the months leading up to our wedding day, we felt like we were running a gauntlet of decision making: What jobs should we take, and when would we start? What city should we move to? What car should we buy? How much are we willing to spend on rent? Where will we go on our honeymoon? What phone and health insurance plans should we choose? What items need to go on our wedding registry?

Not to mention, of course, all of the other hundreds of wedding-related decisions. But there was one decision that weighed heavier than all of the others. It caused the most distress, anxiety, misunderstanding, disagreement, frustration, and conflict. We had discussed it casually when we were dating, but once we got engaged, it became a daily discussion—for months. Even after we made our decision, we contemplated changing our minds every day. The decision was this: *How many people do we want to invite to our wedding? A couple hundred of our closest friends and family members, or the whole world?*

I most definitely never imagined having my wedding aired on national television, but it was. For better, for worse. See what I did there? When we got engaged, we were approached by TV producers, the TLC network, and PR people who were all trying to convince me that filming our wedding for an episode of *Little People, Big World* was a good idea.

Aside from our trip to Costa Rica, I had only been on the show a few times. The production crews hadn't been able to weasel their way into filming much of our dating relationship because our long-distance situation created too great an obstacle. However, once I had the ring on my finger, they were eager to get access to our love story. Given that half of the other shows that air on TLC are wedding-related, saying the network executives were jazzed about the prospect of filming our wedding would be an understatement.

At the time, *Little People, Big World* was in its ninth year of filming. Jeremy's childhood and adolescence had been on display in the living rooms of millions of families around the world. Now he was going to be the first Roloff kid to get married. TLC was not about to miss covering all the details that led up to the big celebration and the first family wedding at Roloff Farms.

In my ignorance, I had always just assumed that once we got

married, Jeremy would leave the TV part of his life behind and we'd start our own life together. I thought the extent of my involvement in filming would consist of merely talking with Jeremy about the effects of growing up on national television. I didn't consider the fact that I might have to join him in the public eye.

So when I was first presented with the option to film our wedding, I quickly shut it down. Even Jeremy wasn't too jazzed on the idea. We didn't like the idea of our wedding becoming a commercialized broadcast event. We didn't want to have to add the time-consuming tasks related to filming our wedding planning because it would be yet another massive commitment on top of our already overwhelming summer. Plus, with the nature of filming and scheduling, we knew it would likely mean we'd end up having to do most things twice. We'd go cake tasting on our own and then film cake tasting, go dress shopping on our own and then film dress shopping, and so on. Both Jeremy and I shared these concerns, but I had a list of my own concerns too.

I knew that the majority of the filming would be heavily dependent on me. Jeremy was still in school in Santa Barbara, so the producers would rely on *me* for filming content for the episodes leading up to our wedding. I knew they'd want to film my bridal shower, dress shopping, hunting for decor, planning the reception, and other meetings with vendors, including Jer's parents, since their backyard was our wedding venue.

Another concern was that I didn't want my family and friends to feel weird or like they couldn't be themselves. It's nerve-racking enough to give a wedding toast, but the pressure of this toast being televised adds a whole new level of jitters. I felt bad about putting my dad, best friend, and sister in that position.

In contrast, Jer's friends and family were used to being filmed.

They had grown up on the show. Furthermore, I didn't want the cameras to make our guests feel uncomfortable. I wanted everyone to feel like they could be themselves. There's nothing quite like a bunch of men and women dressed in black and wearing headsets who are trying to control everything about the way we wanted our wedding to feel—intimate, welcoming, unique, story-driven, and God-centered. Plus, all of our guests would be required to sign a release indicating their willingness to appear on camera. I cringed at the thought of guests at our wedding being greeted with an airport TSA-screening kind of setup, complete with a giant sign that read, "Please refrain from posting pictures," to keep guests from spoiling the episode. *Eye roll!*

Oh, and there were other concerns. I wanted to be able to hang out with my bridesmaids all day, listening to music, dancing, and getting ready together. But guess what. You can't play music when the cameras are rolling because of copyright issues. As I envisioned spending the majority of my wedding day in the bonus room at the farm with all of my bridesmaids, family, and a crew of men I hardly knew watching us with cameras, it didn't exactly sound enjoyable or comfortable. And speaking of uncomfortable, I would also have to wear a cumbersome microphone all day under my wedding dress.

Other production-related concerns included having to redo scenes because the crew missed a shot, getting pulled away from our reception for interviews, the obnoxious China ball lights they'd have to put up when it got dark, and having cameramen in the background of all of our wedding photos. On top of all this, I was stressed about the conflicts I knew would inevitably arise between myself, the TV people, my in-laws who were hosting the wedding, and my father who was graciously paying for it all.

Needless to say, the decision to film our wedding was not an easy one. We spent hours on the phone in our last days of being long distance trying to discern the Lord's will for our decision to film or not to film our wedding. Through countless conversations, counsel, and prayers, we realized there was no right or wrong choice; we simply needed to make a decision and be unified in it. That was the most important thing. We didn't want to allow a disagreement to cause future division and resentment.

So after extensive consideration, we decided to move forward with filming our wedding. You may be thinking, *Ummm, why?* We moved ahead because the show had been such a huge part of Jeremy's life and because it would give us an opportunity to share the gospel through our wedding and to encourage other soon-to-be-married couples to focus more on the marriage than the wedding and more on the promise than the pictures.

As the months passed, many of my concerns became reality. Perhaps the most emotionally taxing reality was the drama and conflict between us and our parents, us and the TV network, and between the two of us. The process was so stressful and demanding that one day Jeremy and I just broke down crying. We still didn't have jobs or a place to live; we were fighting about Kate; Jeremy's parents were going through a separation; my parents were very frustrated by the filming process; and we were emotionally over-whelmed by everything we were processing in premarital counseling. Jeremy was also having a heck of a time trying to keep the TV crew from encroaching on the parts of our wedding day I wanted to keep private. I felt incapacitated by stress, and Jeremy was starting to feel like everything was his fault.

I held him as he sobbed and choked out through gasping breaths, "I ruined our wedding. This is all my fault. I'm sorry. We never should have said yes to filming." Yes, this was the same cryfest we had earlier when we were reconciling the Kate situation. I could tell he was genuinely sorry, and it hurt my heart to see him so broken. I cried with him. I assured him that despite all the things that had gone or could go wrong, I would never hold this decision over his head. It was *our* decision, and we were unified in it. No matter what!

This was yet another test of oneness, and through it I began to realize how stubborn and unsupportive I had been in connection with something that had been such an integral part of Jeremy's life. When it came to filming, I was not adhering to the principle of sharing. I sensed the Lord drawing my attention to how discouraging and resistant I was being, and my heart slowly started to soften toward this part of Jer's life. *What if my opposition is shutting a God-opened door? Maybe I need to just accept that this is a part of my future husband's life. Rather than being combative, maybe I could be welcoming.*

Instead of viewing filming as an inconvenient and stressful intrusion, I began to focus on the beautiful opportunity of filming our wedding. Most of my concerns had a shortsighted purpose—having our wedding day be exactly as I wanted. However, we ended up saying yes to filming our wedding for a larger purpose—reflecting the gospel to millions of people through our promise. I began to trust that God was in the decision to film our wedding and that he was bigger than my concerns and fears.

Now, instead of fighting it, I embraced the opportunity to share our love story with the world in hopes that viewers would catch a glimpse of the gospel. We would be able to encourage our generation to prepare more for their marriage than their wedding. We would have the story of our wedding day recorded to watch again and share with our children and grandchildren.

In the end, the experience of our wedding day was immeasurably more than I could have ever asked for or imagined. Jeremy worked so hard to communicate my requests for privacy and to protect the personal moments between us. He also drew a hard line with the production crew that we would not redo anything—no second takes. They would simply be invited to capture our wedding day as it unfolded, but they would not have a hand in *how* it unfolded.

For the most part, the crew respected our wishes and worked hard to accommodate our concerns. In the end, they did a great job. I acknowledged that I was holding too tightly to how my wedding might be perceived instead of thanking God for the man I was about to receive. Filming our wedding forced us to loosen the reins of control and allowed our day to be more about becoming one than obsessing over all the little details.

The decision to film our wedding was a great test of our oneness, and we passed! I sincerely believe the Lord blessed our determination to pursue oneness each step of the way. And although the journey to "I do" was more stressful and challenging than we had anticipated, God's blessing transformed all the hardships into an unforgettable wedding day, a beautiful marriage, and a book to tell the story.

JEREMY

The evening air was warm as Audrey and I sat at a table on the pool deck, enjoying the shade of the farm's hundred-year-old walnut tree. A gentle breeze was swaying the tire swing as the sun speckled through the dancing leaves onto our faces. We had just finished a long list of wedding to-dos for the day, and we were looking forward to a relaxing evening and forgetting the wedding for a few hours.

I glanced around and took in the beauty that is the farm. The big red barn stood stoic and strong amid the grass and the apple tree. The air was thick with light from the summer dust, and the bugs looked like tiny glowing orbs with the setting sun to their backs. We both let out a big sigh of relief and contentment. Just as I reached for the bottle of wine we had picked for the evening, I heard the barn door creek open, and I saw the film crew walking toward us, loaded with all their gear. I wondered what they were doing when it hit me—we still had scene work to do for the day. Audrey put her head down on the table in exhaustion. We were both emotionally tapped out and had our hearts set on quietly drinking a glass of wine and watching the sunset twice—once as it fell behind the barn and then relocating to watch it set again behind the coastal mountain range.

Our hopes for the evening ended abruptly, and I realized it was my fault. I had forgotten about our scene work. As soon as we began filming, something was off between us. I could tell Audrey was bummed and not in the mood to film. Neither was I. We were scheduled to talk about several important topics—our move after the wedding, when our parents could visit us, and what we still had to do before the wedding.

As the scene work progressed, it was clear we weren't connecting. We both reverted to our usual approach for dealing with stress and conflict—I got quiet, and Audrey got snappy. We were getting mad at each other because it was easier than getting mad at our circumstances.

In a flash of brilliance, I reached over and grabbed Audrey's hand. To my surprise, it worked! My heart softened, and I felt Audrey's do the same. Immediately, we remembered that we were on the same team. We looked at each other in a silent gaze of understanding and decided to finish with competence the work we had to do.

You may be wondering, *What the heck are you talking about, Jer? What worked?* Well, a few weeks previously, Chris and Jamie had given us a secret weapon for pursuing oneness and keeping conflict under control—holding hands. This was our first opportunity to try it.

Before you roll your eyes and flip the page, hear me out. Have you ever tried to be angry at someone while holding his or her hand? It's hard—try it! When conflict comes, lean into the counsel of the apostle Paul: "If it is possible, as far as it depends on you, live at peace with everyone" (Romans 12:18). Do your part to build the peace. Grab your beloved's hand and pursue oneness. When I reached over to grab Audrey's hand, my pride crumbled and her heart softened. With a single, silent action, we both remembered we were on the same team and had the same goal.

When I think about a successful team, I think about unity, oneness, and a shared vision. A team will always perform better when players treat each other as teammates, not opponents. Adopting a teammate perspective is what enabled us to shift into filming with unity and oneness. When conflict arose and threatened to divide our oneness, we held hands as a reminder of our shared goal.

I think most people would probably affirm the idea of marriage as a team effort, but marriage isn't just any type of team. Marriage is a *covenant* team. Both players are completely committed—there is no plan B, no free agents, and no trading windows. A covenant is a promise to love sacrificially, to do whatever it takes to make your relationship work.

Every team has an objective—a shared mission, dream, or purpose. Can you imagine getting a team together and saying, "We're a team!" but failing to identify what it is you're supposed to do?

That's a team that won't last very long. Yet many of us enter into marriage that way. We fail to identify our shared mission. A team with a shared mission can't entirely eliminate conflict, but it can turn situations doomed to escalated conflict into opportunities for healthy growth.

We believe that the point of marriage is not limited to the marriage itself. Rather, marriage is a vehicle through which we get to participate in something bigger, the grand plan of a mighty God. When a marriage has a vision beyond itself, it can accomplish amazing things—just as teams do when they're united around a vision.

For Christ followers, this vision starts with reflecting the gospel by living out the sacrificial love of Jesus. In that sense, a Christian marriage may be the first version of the gospel that many people will see. Beyond this, a couple may have a mission together that takes the form of a ministry, business, or social cause. Raising children who love and serve the Lord is a mission; so is deciding to pay off your house, volunteering, and planning a trip. All of these can be shared missions—some long-term, some short-term. Every team has something it's working toward, and the strength of the team is in the oneness with which they pursue it.

Here's an illustration that demonstrates how important this is. Imagine there are three ships at sea, each with its own crew. The first ship has a crew with a vision to reach the Americas—that's their mission. So they wake up every morning eager to get to work. Because they are unified in their goal, they are eager to learn more about how to work best as a team to accomplish that goal. They can easily measure their progress because they know exactly what they hope to achieve. They are also able to effectively manage their resources because they agree to use them for accomplishing their goal.

The second ship has no shared vision. They simply wake up, see which way the wind is blowing, and let what happens happen. They make no measurable progress because there is no goal to measure progress against. It's impossible for them to know if they're successful because they don't know what they're trying to accomplish. They argue about how to manage resources because there's no agreement about what they should be used for. So the crew on this boat fights constantly about what they're doing and where they're headed.

And then there is the third ship—one with a split crew. Half of the crew want to sail to the Americas, and the other half want to sail to Asia. They're divided. You can probably already imagine the conflict on this ship when it comes to making any decisions about their objective and the use of resources.

It's not hard to see the implications this illustration has for relationships and marriage, right? Is your relationship mission-minded, mission-divided, or missionless?

By the time Audrey and I decided to film our wedding, we were united in our decision and trusting that the Lord would use our decision for his purposes. Being united in the decision enabled us to focus more on having a healthy marriage than a happy wedding. In the process, we gained a vital tool—holding hands—to help us remember that we're on the same team and share the same vision and mission.

To this day, Audrey and I sit down at the beginning of every year and talk about what our goal for the year is. This year, it was writing a book—this book. Last year, it was buying a house. The year before that, we started a ministry called Beating50Percent. Every year, we make sure we know what we're working toward as a team and where our resources are going.

We're currently working on creating our family mission, which will serve as our broad, overall mission, a kind of road map for decision making. We hope that by establishing the pillars of our family mission, we will be able to cross-examine opportunities with the pillars of our family mission. It's a work in progress, but we're excited for the day when we can hang it on a wall in our home.

* * *

Once we were engaged, we made sure we were one in all of our decisions. We were intentional about becoming one with our language, our possessions, and our resources. On our wedding day, we took the next steps toward oneness when we committed our lives to one another and consummated our union, becoming one in body and spirit.

Speaking of consummation, do I even need to say how important sex is for building oneness in marriage? Sex unifies two people. This is why sex is so powerful within marriage and can be so destructive outside of it. When we share sexual oneness with someone without the foundation of a marriage commitment to support it, our love is deeply vulnerable.

Once we were married, we continued to learn that becoming one is a daily choice. In the words of writer Annie Dillard, "How we spend our days is, of course, how we spend our lives."[1] Behind every gold medal is a journey of sacrifice and discipline; behind every summited mountain is a trail of training; behind every successful business is a path of persevering through failure; and behind every healthy, long-lasting marriage is a lifestyle of sacrifice for the sake of oneness. It is our everyday, sometimes seemingly insignificant decisions that sow either seeds of separateness or of oneness.

11

PROTECT
Your Love

JEREMY

Audrey and I met unexpectedly on January 16, 2010. Under a brick archway, she opened the door, and I saw her for the first time, speckled with mud and sweat, shimmering in the glow of the streetlight. Our love story began in that doorway. Over the next two years, we fell in love, deeper and deeper, until we had something we couldn't imagine losing—each other. After three years of doing long distance, we promised to love each other for better or for worse, till death do us part. Ever since our wedding day, we've been living out that promise and continuing to pursue a love story worth reading one day.

Auj and I still consider ourselves to be in the early chapters of a love story that we never want to end. However, as we look at the world around us, it's quite clear that love, if not protected, often does not endure. Sooner or later, most of us are touched by failed love. We have parents who divorce, close friends who couldn't seem to make it work, or our own heartbreaking experiences. We have to reckon with the fact that if love is something we can fall into, it is something we can fall out of. If we don't protect it, our love story can suffer an unhappy ending.

We've all heard it said, "Fifty percent of marriages end in divorce." Although the actual numbers may vary slightly, this is a shocking estimate. The actual divorce rate is a difficult metric to measure because of all the unmeasurable and unreported variables involved. However, even if it's in the ballpark, this should be a call to arms for everyone who desires a love that lasts.

Throughout each chapter of this book, we've shared different ways we've pursued and protected our love story—through patience, unhindered time, community, demolishing walls, creative pursuit, pursuing the Lord, communicating our needs, being willing to change, the principle of sharing, managing our expectations, our code of conflict, purity, wise counsel, illuminating the past, and reconciliation. Of all the different ways we seek to safeguard our love, three things have stood out as pillars of protection—boundaries, rhythms, and prayer.

Boundaries as Protection

Authors Henry Cloud and John Townsend define a boundary as "a property line."[1] One of the functions of healthy boundaries is to protect the "property" of our relationship from trespassing. In *Boundaries in Marriage*, Cloud and Townsend write, "While many dynamics go into producing and maintaining love, over and over again one issue is at the top of the list: boundaries. When boundaries are not established in the beginning of a marriage, or when they break down, marriages break down as well . . . For this intimacy to develop and grow, there must be boundaries."[2]

As Audrey and I entered into marriage, we knew that the locomotive of our love would not stay on track without boundaries. Boundaries are the protective rail lines of our love. Boundaries are designed to *protect*, not prohibit. For example, a ski boundary line, a divider on a freeway, directions on the back of a medication bottle—these boundaries are not set in place to hold us back; they are set in place to safeguard us.

Boundaries in marriage are no different. Their purpose is to protect our marriages from division, hurt, bitterness, animosity, and miscommunication. Early on in our marriage, Auj and I were encouraged to protect our love by setting boundaries for our finances, our friendships, and our technology—specifically social media.

I believe that the overuse of social media is posing a massive threat to our love stories. It can be a tempting place to zone out, escape, or invite wandering eyes. It can allow comparison to steal the joy that our love stories were meant to experience. It can steal our time, causing us to spend more of it scrolling feeds than connecting with our loved ones. Without boundaries for phone and social media use, we'll lose our grip on what it means to truly connect.

Here are a few of the boundaries we use to protect our love story:

- We don't use social media on Sunday.
- We don't check our phone during date night.
- We don't get on our phones in bed.
- We have access to each other's social media accounts.
- We don't go out one-on-one (coffee/drinks) with the opposite sex.

- We don't keep texts, emails, or social media messages to the opposite sex a secret.
- We don't text old boyfriends/girlfriends without the other knowing about it.

We encourage you to come up with your own list of boundaries. It doesn't need to be exhaustive, nor does it need to be completed overnight. Just begin the conversation for the sake of protecting your love.

Rhythms as Protection

Rhythms are constant and reliable. They are a way to build consistent patterns of behavior for successful outcomes. Rhythms have been monumental in our marriage for protecting our love. The rhythm of date night, taking an annual trip, keeping a sabbath, putting our phones away at certain times, working out, nightly walks—all are life rhythms of consistency that help us work toward the life and marriage we want.

You know that famous quote, "Failing to plan is planning to fail"? I believe the same is true with rhythms. Throughout the years of our marriage, we've established daily rhythms, weekly rhythms, and yearly rhythms. We have implemented rhythms for rest, rhythms for health, rhythms for family, rhythms for celebration, and rhythms for communication. Some have come and gone with certain seasons of life, but some are constant across all seasons. We've noticed that all the folks who have marriages we look up to have rhythms—consistent patterns of behavior that they can rely on.

After seeing how vital and helpful healthy rhythms are, we decided to make our motto for this year "the art of rhythm." Every year, our family focuses on something to work on. Last year it was "the art of saying no." This year, we focused on healthy rhythms and how to live with consistent patterns of behavior that produce the life we want. If there is one rhythm that has had the most impact on our love story, it has been our weekly rhythm for connecting and communicating with each other—our marriage journal.

The number one piece of marriage advice we got during our wedding season was "communicate, communicate, communicate!" Some couples are naturally gifted at this—bless them! For the rest of us, communication comes with a learning curve and requires practice.

In an effort to lay the groundwork for healthy communication in our marriage, we committed during our honeymoon to asking ourselves a series of questions once a week. The questions were simple but incredibly effective for cultivating consistent, clear, and honest communication. We committed to asking each other the same six questions every week for the first year of our marriage. This weekly rhythm helped us understand each other better so we could love each other better. It was so helpful for us that first year that we committed to continuing the rhythm.

A couple of years ago, we developed and self-published this weekly rhythm into a journal—*The Marriage Journal*—with the hope of helping other couples connect, communicate, and grow in love. The basis of *The Marriage Journal* is six questions that we ask one another and record our answers to. Each week also has its own short, encouraging devotional and a calendar to help you and your spouse get on the same page before you head into the week. At the end of each journal session, we end our time in prayer, which has helped establish a rhythm for prayer in our marriage as well. *The Marriage Journal* is a rhythm that has been the gift that keeps on giving, and I feel like I could write an entire book about all that it's done for our marriage, but this is not that book.

Prayer as Protection

I've heard it said that one of the truest tests of our love for someone is how often and fervently we pray for them. In other words, prayer is evidence of love. If you're married, do you pray for your spouse? Do you pray *with* your spouse? An experienced married couple challenged Audrey and me a few years ago when they asked us, "When you encounter conflict in your marriage, do you pray about it more than you talk about it?" This statement still convicts us today.

I've heard it said that our relationship with God is only as strong as our prayer life. Prayer is a relationship, a conversation, an ordering of our worship. I love this quote from Charles Spurgeon: "True prayer is neither a mere mental exercise nor a vocal performance. It is far deeper than that—it is spiritual transaction with the Creator of heaven and earth."[3]

For us, praying *together* has increased our intimacy, our faith, our connectedness, our dreams, our vision, our direction, and our love. Praying together has brought *unity* and *connectedness*; Satan wants to bring division and detachment. Praying together has been a way to *partner with God*; Satan tempts us to believe we don't need God's partnership. Praying together brings *God's truth and will into the light*; Satan wants us to walk in the darkness of lies. Praying together offers a *testimony to God's faithfulness* as we see our prayers being answered; Satan wants to blind us from the way God is working in our life and marriage. Praying together keeps our lives *focused and in tune with the Holy Spirit*; Satan wants us to fall asleep or get distracted by something else.

We believe that prayer is the best first line of defense when we encounter struggles, issues of the heart, and conflict. It should be our go-to, not our last resort. Pray for each other, for your future marriage and family, for your discernment in decisions, for the Lord to guide your relationship, for your dreams and desires, for life circumstances, for growth in your knowledge of the truth, for the ability to walk in wisdom, for a heart that longs to praise God, and for protection over your love story. I love how Tim Keller describes the value of prayer:

> Prayer is the only entryway into genuine self-knowledge. It is also the main way we experience deep change—the reordering of our loves. Prayer is how God gives us so many of the unimaginable things he has for us. Indeed, prayer makes it safe for God to give us many of the things we most desire. It is the way we know God, the way we finally treat God *as* God. Prayer is simply the key to everything we need to do and be in life.[4]

One simple way you can pray protection over your love story is by praying the armor of God (Ephesians 6:13–17) over your loved one while inserting their name. For example:

> *Father God, thank you for giving me Audrey to love. In an effort to love her better, I want to pray your armor over her. Would you place on Audrey's head the helmet of salvation to guard her thoughts and mind in Christ. Place on her chest the breastplate of righteousness to guard her heart and keep it pure. Wrap around her waist the belt of truth to prevent any lies from creeping into her thoughts or head and to keep her far from temptation. Put the sandals of peace on her feet to keep her walking bravely and courageously without fear or*

worry. Give her the shield of faith to trust in your leading. Lord, train her in the sword of the Spirit to fight against the fiery arrows of attack. Cover her with your full protection and armor as she enters the battlefield today. In Jesus' name. Amen.

We realize that someone may read this chapter and say, "Well, I don't set boundaries, establish rhythms, or pray, and my relationship is fine!" Well, I passed my SAT and said the same thing to all the kids who spent hours studying for it, but I took a risk, and some would call it a foolish one. Just because it worked doesn't mean it was smart. I imagine the hurt of failed love isn't worth the risk. We don't put our seat belt on when we need it; we put it on before we need it. The same should be true for protecting our love. Don't wait until your marriage or relationship has crashed to protect it. It's much easier to protect it than to put it back together.

Ultimately, we believe that the greatest protector of love is God: "If God is for us, who can be against us?" (Romans 8:31). And God is love: "Whoever does not love does not know God, because God is love" (1 John 4:8). As we invite God into our love story and allow him to be the strand that prevents us from unraveling (Ecclesiastes 4:12), we are able to love more intentionally, more creatively, and more faithfully.

We're all in the process of writing a love story. Maybe you're dating and have just begun the first chapter. Maybe you're married and on chapter 15. Or maybe you're single and writing an exciting prologue. Wherever you are in your love story, protect it. Be intentional, get creative, and stay faithful.

IDEAS FOR PROTECTING YOUR MARRIAGE

- Protect your marriage by spending time alone with God daily.
- Protect your marriage by never speaking poorly of your spouse to others.
- Protect your marriage through sex.
- Protect your marriage through wise counsel (or professional counsel, if necessary).
- Protect your marriage by finding a community that holds you accountable, encourages you, and prays for you.
- Protect your marriage by safeguarding your relationships with friends of the opposite sex.
- Protect your marriage by prioritizing your relationship with your spouse over all other relationships.
- Protect your marriage through intentional weekly check-in times (using *The Marriage Journal* as a guide, for example) and through consistent communication.
- Protect your marriage by setting boundaries in the workplace and on outside activities in general.
- Protect your marriage through the principle of sharing.
- Protect your marriage with honesty. No secrets.
- Protect your marriage by doing the little things.
- Protect your marriage by praying for your marriage and your spouse.
- Protect your marriage by establishing phone/social media boundaries.

THE BIG DAY

AUDREY

I wasn't one of those girls who spent every moment of her childhood dreaming about her wedding day. I knew I wanted to get married outside on a farm, and I knew I wanted to write my own vows, but that was about it. In adolescence, however, I spent a fair amount of time dreaming about my ideal love story. I wanted a husband who was humble and kind, who made me feel pursued and protected. I wanted a husband who loved God and led us spiritually. I wanted a husband who would cherish me and challenge me. I wanted a husband who would be my best friend. In Jeremy, I got exceedingly more than I could ever have asked for or imagined in a husband. He was, and continues to become, the man I dreamed about and prayed for.

As our wedding day approached, I was very clear about one thing: I didn't want our wedding to be about the party, the pictures, and the people; I wanted it to be about the promise. During our engagement, we made a commitment to each other to spend more time preparing for our marriage than our wedding, and we wanted our wedding day to reflect that pledge. I wanted our wedding to be a day of worship and a proclamation of God's love, not just our love. So we added meaning to every detail we could as a reminder to ourselves and everyone in attendance that this day was about a covenant, not a contract. About a promise, not a party—even though it was still a raging good party!

I waited until the night before our wedding to write my vows because I wanted to be as emotionally present as possible when I recorded my forever promises. Pausing every now and then to pray, I tried to articulate my vows in a creative, specific, and God-centered way. I stayed up late, scribbling the expressions of my heart and declaring my promise to love Jeremy "from this day forward." Every few minutes, I'd get a "one more sleep!" text with a bunch of wedding emojis from one of my friends. I smiled in the anticipation of waking up next to Jeremy for the rest of my life. Tomorrow we would start our forever.

One month prior to our wedding, my parents sold the house my siblings and I had grown up in and moved to a farm out in the country. They had always said that once my siblings and I graduated from high school, they would move out to the country because they loved it. My younger brother had graduated that summer, so they were on the hunt for a little plot of land. And get this—they ended up buying the property that looks down on our trestle! The spot where Jeremy and I got engaged is now just a few feet from my parents' property line! All this to say that on the morning of our wedding, I woke up to the sound of the train and the majestic view of our beloved trestle.

The morning of our wedding, I felt like I had always felt on race days—nervous and bursting with adrenaline, and I had no appetite. My heart was racing, but at the same time, I had never felt more at peace. I decided to go for a short prayer walk down to our trestle. When I reached the base of the bridge, I sat in the grass and recorded a video of myself praying for our wedding and marriage.

The video began with me saying something like, "How cool is it that I can sit here on the morning of our wedding and pray for our marriage in the spot where our love story began!" Then I proceeded to praise God and pray for protection and his presence over our day and our marriage. I sent the video to Jeremy with an "I love you" text and put my phone on airplane mode for the rest of the day.

As I was walking back to my parents' house, I started thinking about our future daughter, and how the next time I would experience something of this magnitude would be on her wedding day. Then I got a Holy Spirit nudge to act on those thoughts. For some reason, I felt very strongly that I was supposed to write a letter on *my* wedding day to give to my future daughter on *her* wedding day.

When I got back to the house, my whole family was in wedding hustle mode. I was so thankful I'd gotten up early enough to steal away for some time with the Lord in the quiet under our trestle. If I hadn't gone for that walk, I would have missed the nudge to write the letter to my future daughter.

I piled all the wedding things in my car and headed to Roloff Farms, just a short three-minute drive away. When I arrived, there were people, trucks, vendors, and camera crews everywhere. I smiled as I passed them, leaving the chaos to my family and the vendors while I sought shelter in the farmhouse with my bridesmaids.

As we started getting ready, I spent some time writing my letter to our future daughter. I remember thinking, *What if I only have boys?* But that didn't stop my mission. I wrote about all the things I was feeling and tried to comfort, encourage, and celebrate with my girl by relating to her future emotions through my current ones. I wanted my daughter to know how I felt on the day I married her father. *Whoa!*

In the letter, I prayed for her future husband, their wedding day, and their marriage. It was a wild experience. It felt as if I were writing to someone I knew and yet was someone who was still unknown to the world. I ended by letting her know that by the time she read the letter, Jeremy and I would have been praying for both her and her beloved for a long time.

Our day seemed to be marked by letters. By the time I finished writing my letter to our future daughter, Jeremy's brother Zach and a couple of the other groomsmen knocked on the bonus room door and entered, bearing a gift and a letter from Jeremy. The letter was written on his typewriter, of course. The gift was a custom brand with our initials on it in the shape of a heart. Yes, my husband got me a cattle brand as our wedding gift. You're probably chuckling, but I was fighting back tears. Especially when I read this line in Jeremy's letter: "Today will brand our love in permanence." In exchange, I handed the guys my gift for Jer, along with a letter I had written on my typewriter.

Shortly after our letter exchange, I went to see Jeremy for our first look. If you watched our wedding on TV, you wouldn't know we had done this because it was just Jeremy and me in the forest with our wedding photographer. We stood just a few steps away from the campfire pit that had kindled and illuminated our love story. When I walked up from behind and tapped him on the shoulder, Jeremy turned around and gasped. "You're beautiful, babe," he said. "And the dress, it's just what you wanted. I love it." I'm not a fairy-tale princess kind of girl, but in that moment, I sure did feel like one.

The rest of our wedding day was saturated with story and symbolism. I wanted everything about our wedding to tell our love story—from the typewritten letters to the red lipstick on the dessert plates, and everything in between. As I thought about walking down the aisle, I envisioned myself holding a sign with a message on it, something Jeremy could read as I walked toward him. As I explored that thought, I realized that brides usually carry bouquets—and I should probably do that—but the groomsmen didn't have to carry anything. They could carry my message for me!

I texted each of the groomsmen and explained that I was crafting a surprise for Jeremy during our wedding ceremony and I needed their help. Then I asked each of them to send me one or two words they had heard Jeremy use to describe me. I said that the words could be silly or serious. They each texted me back a word or two, although I had no idea what some of them even meant (I'm sure they were inside jokes), but I knew Jeremy would know.

These were their responses, and they became the words on the signs the groomsmen carried as they walked down the aisle: *fiery fox*, *sexy rapsy*, *Daisy Braids*, *pure joy*, *tough*, *passionate*, *my wife*, *determined*, *train-tracksy*, *babe*, and *Auj*. I had the ring bearer carry a sign that read, "and now," and my dad carried a sign that read, "she's yours," as we walked arm in arm down the aisle.

When I finally reached the end of the aisle, I held tightly to Jeremy's hands with tears of joy in my eyes. Chris Herb, who was officiating, asked Jeremy and me to turn around and look at the family and friends who had gathered together to witness our union. This is such a vivid moment engraved in my memory. It was an incredible blessing to see the smiling faces of all the people who had encouraged, supported, and prayed for Jeremy and me during our years of courting. It made me all the more excited to proclaim my promises to Jeremy in front of all of them.

During the ceremony, Chris gave us a precious gift—a little plank of wood from our trestle with a personalized plaque on it that read:

THE ROLOFFS—EST. 2014
NEW TRACKS
GOD. EACH OTHER. OTHERS.

As he handed us the gift, he explained to our family and friends how the train tracks symbolized our love story, and how it was the place we would go to cast vision and dream of our future together. His prayer and blessing over us was that we would always seek to lay new tracks with the Lord, with each other, and with others. It was such a perfect and powerful gift that spoke volumes about our love story. We beamed with gratitude as we received the gift, excited to hang it in our home as a daily reminder.

Then Chris gave us another gift. During our premarital counseling, he had asked Jeremy and me to write a list of ten things we loved about each other. We weren't allowed to tell each other what we had written, so the first time we heard them was during our wedding ceremony as Chris read them aloud. Coincidentally, Jeremy and I had the same number—ten—which brought enormous grins to our freckled faces.

TEN THINGS I LOVE ABOUT JEREMY

1. His patient and persistent pursuit of me.
2. His passionate faithfulness to the Lord and to me.
3. His mannerisms. All of them. They are unlike any human. [I laugh.]
4. His ability to make me feel safe and secure all the time.
5. His craving for adventure and eagerness to explore.
6. The way he looks at me and tells me I'm pretty every day.

7. His ability to build, create, and innovate and the way he inspires others and me.
8. His willingness to change and the way he strives to be more and do more.
9. The way he puts my insecurities to sleep and constantly builds my trust.
10. The freckles on his upper lip.

TEN THINGS I LOVE ABOUT AUDREY

1. Her passion for life. The want to do things.
2. The back hair curl that never quite makes it into the bun.
3. Her cooking abilities and my appreciation when she prepares food for me.
4. The way she loves Jesus.
5. How she treats me when I'm stressed.
6. Her beautiful, joy-filled smile.
7. Her heart for others.
8. How she gets excited about farm things.
9. Her physique.
10. The lip freckles that always come out in the sun.

After Chris read our lists, we exchanged vows.

Jeremy's Vows

Audrey Mirabella Roloff, my beautiful bride,

Today, I take your hand and commit myself to you. My heart is full of joy and I want you to know that there is not a doubt in my mind that God's is too.

I commit myself to our mission. To be your teammate, lay down my pride, and practice self-submission.

I vow to stand by you in sickness, to be ahead of you in trials, behind you in support, and with you in joy.

Audrey, I am yours.

Audrey Mirabella Botti, to you I vow my service. For completion of who you are to be. Love of my life, a kingdom warrior with aid to set the world free.

I promise to love the new you every year.

I promise to pursue you in all of your beauty.

You are the strongest person I know. You inspire me, teach me, support me, and excite me.

To begin a life with you and live out the years is what I was built to do. My confidence in this through prayer and desire has extinguished all of the fears.

I vow to listen to your heart and to give you mine.

Audrey Mirabella Botti, finally, I make you mine.

Audrey's Vows

Babe, as I stand here about to take your hand for life, I am reminded of the poem you wrote me once in a letter during our three years of long distance. It was a short and simple note that read, "Like a butterfly to the cage, stomach flies to the emotional rage." You still give my stomach butterflies when I see you. Whether it's for the first time in three months or the first time in three hours.

My heart beats slower and faster at the same time. Everything about me wants to express my love for you. My love for you is more than just a feeling of in-loveness; it's an unwavering confidence in my choice to love you with all that I am for the rest of my life. I want to love you in direct, personal, specific, and ever-fresh ways. There is no doubt in my mind that you are the one I am supposed to team up with for life. I know the Lord is rejoicing with us today, and fist pumping at his successful matchmaking skills.

I thank God relentlessly for giving me a man I don't deserve. You are that man. You have all the characteristics of the husband I prayed for, and who filled my journal pages during the years leading up to meeting you. You are above and beyond what I could have ever asked or imagined. Because of your great love for me, today I make this great promise to you:

- I promise to be on your team for life.
- I promise to be your biggest fan.
- I promise to support you with all my heart, soul, mind, and strength.
- I promise to affirm you in public and in private.
- I promise to be your prayer warrior.
- I promise to put God first.

- I promise to put you before anyone and anything else.
- I promise to always let you drive.
- I promise to push the envelope.
- I promise to rub your neck when you're stressed.
- I promise to scratch your head when you're tired.
- I promise to motivate and challenge you to live up to the calling you have received.
- I promise to keep my bathroom clean.
- I promise to ask you hard questions and hold you accountable.
- I promise to humbly and selflessly serve you.
- I promise to be faithful.
- I promise to continue writing you notes and letters.
- I promise to commit to date night.
- I promise to be quick to forgive.
- I promise to be better with directions.
- I promise to take care of you when you're sick.
- I promise to tame down my redhead stubbornness.
- I promise to respect you and honor you.
- I promise to follow you and trust you.
- I promise to love you always, always more.

Like I always do, I couldn't help but write these words on my hand on my wedding day: "ALWAYS MORE." Our wedding is about far more than a day in a dress; it's about you and me becoming one by the powerful grace of God. It's a picture of the love that Christ has for us.

I hope that our love will forever reflect that image—the image of Christ's undeniable love for all of us. But I also write these words on my hand as a reminder that by Christ's strength, there are always more ways that I can serve you, more things to learn about you, more grace to grant you, more humility to have toward you, more support to offer you, more laughter to share with you, more children to give you, more adventure to seek with you, more passion to share with you, more faith to have in you, more places to go with you, more people to meet with you, more prayers to pray with you, more ways to worship with you, and more love to give to you.

Today, I make the most important decision of my life, second to deciding to follow Jesus. Today, I become your wife—finally! You light me up, Jeremy. I want to be part of all the exciting changes in your life. I want to be holding your hand as we embark on future adventures together. I know it will be work, but I'm willing to run the extra mile every day for you, babe. I believe in God's calling on your life, and I can't stand the thought of missing out on it. Let's braid it for life, babe—Christ, you, and I. I love you forever.

Your Daisy Braids

Before we walked back down the aisle as Mr. and Mrs. Roloff, we walked into the tiny farm church in front of which we were married and had an intimate intermission before our big celebration. We wanted our first act as a married couple to be taking Communion. It was a beautiful moment of recognizing our oneness with Christ and our new oneness with one another. We came before our Lord in holy surrender, abundant thanksgiving, and immeasurable joy. We prayed together for the first time as husband and wife and gave thanks to God for orchestrating our love story. As we took the bread and cup, we asked God to continue to write our love story, "till death do us part."

During our wedding reception we took a similar moment of pause together. While everyone was enjoying the reception, we snuck away to a quiet corner and marveled at all of our loved ones who had joined together in celebration of our covenant. We hugged each other and practically said in unison, "Lock it in." Our wedding photographer captured the moment, and it will always be one of my favorite photos.

Our big day was full of blessings, joy, celebration, and love. We didn't want it to end, but we were encouraged that even though the day was ending, our marriage had just begun! Moments before we walked through a tunnel of sparklers to our getaway car, it caught my eye. That typewriter. The typewriter Jeremy used to write me love letters and poems. The typewriter that revealed the words, "Will you marry me?" The typewriter that made our relationship more meaningful and memorable than we ever imagined it could be. It will always carry such valiant symbolism in our marriage. To this day, it sits on the entryway table in our home, reminding us to continue writing our love letter life and reminding us of this truth: to find and still seek, now that is love.

THE LETTER
Lives On

As we wrote this book, we prayed fervently that it would inspire, encourage, motivate, and challenge you to write a committed, courageous, creative, compelling, and continuous love story. We hope that our story awakens your desire to pursue a love that reflects the thoughtfulness, intention, and beauty of a hand-typed letter. Our journey to "I do" was far from perfect, but we hope it has inspired you to prepare for, pursue, and protect your love as you write your own love letter life.

We no longer face the challenges of a long-distance relationship, but like anyone, our love is vulnerable to growing distant over time. Our promise to one another is that we will never stop pursuing a love letter life. We want our life together to resemble a love letter—thoughtful, timeless, beautifully written, and impossible to delete.

One of the many ways we've continued to write our love story is through anniversary letters. On the last day of our honeymoon, we wrote letters to each other on the beach and sealed them with the intent to read them for the first time on our one-year wedding anniversary. We wanted to remind ourselves of the emotions, thoughts, and stories that filled our lives shortly after getting married.

One year later, on our anniversary, we opened and read them together out loud. We were thankful we had taken the time to write them and were brought to tears as we reminisced about our first year of marriage. Reading our letters out loud was such a fun, romantic, and beautiful experience that we decided to continue the tradition of writing anniversary letters to each other. Every year when we read our letters, we are reminded of what the Lord has brought us through and what he has brought us to. In a way, the story of our lives is recorded through our anniversary love letters. They document the continuation of our love letter life.

Our typewriter has remained on display in every place we've lived since being married. It will always hold profound symbolism. It inspires us to continue living our lives with purpose, intention, and care, just like a hand-typed letter. Although we don't use it much anymore, on February 22, 2017, we decided to load the ink rolls once again to write a different kind of letter—a letter to all of our friends and family on the interwebs. We recorded a little video of us typing it out: "September 2017 . . . WE ARE HAVING A BABY!"

In the weeks leading up to the birth of our first child, we thought it was only fitting to write our unborn daughter a letter. So we each wrote letters expressing our hopes and dreams for our baby girl. We decided it would be the first of many letters we'd write to her each year on her birthday. Eventually, we'll compile them for her to read, perhaps when she gets married and I give her the letter I wrote to her on my wedding day.

On September 10, 2017, we met our daughter, Ember Jean Roloff, for the first time. Our love story grew around the embers of the campfire pit, so we thought it was only fitting to name our first daughter after the place that set our love on fire. After all, she is the fruit of our love.

As we held our daughter for the first time, we prayed over her life and the story she will write. We even prayed for her future husband. Our hope for her is that she will one day write her own beautiful love story—a story full of adventure, passion, and faithfulness. We entrusted her to the Lord and asked him to prepare her heart and her future husband's heart for a love story that will spark hope in the hearts of anyone who comes close to it.

Our prayer for Ember is that she'll be a light in the darkness, glowing in all she does, enduring, fierce, and hard to extinguish— and we hope these same traits remain embedded in our love story: that our love story sheds light, endures through the stormy winds, continues to grow and glow, and ignites a spark in the souls of everyone who encounters it. We commit to always believing in the *more* God has for us—the *more* of him that we get to discover, experience, and love. He is truly the author of our story. We simply hope to be faithful narrators for the rest of our lives.

Love, Jer and Auj

ACKNOWLEDGMENTS

Thank you—

Bryan Norman, for your persistence all those years ago! You've become a good friend, and we couldn't imagine this process without you. See you in Nashville!

Chris and Jamie Herb, for your mentorship and wisdom. We truly look up to your marriage more than you know.

Cendi Botti, for always reading our writings and offering creative, helpful, and encouraging feedback. We love you!

Mitch and Kelsey Chillcott, for pressuring us into that blind date all those years ago.

Alicia Kasen, you have poured your heart and soul into every smallest detail and biggest decision regarding this book. You've made this process more than we ever imagined and are so appreciative of all your hard work.

Carolyn McCready, for believing wholeheartedly in us and in this book from the beginning. We couldn't have dreamed of a better editor and are so beyond grateful for you!

Our family in Bend—the Jacobsons, the Partridges, the Smiths, the Mehans, the Tolpins, and the Farrises—for all the support, encouragement and advice. You've been one of the best things that's ever happened to us. See you all soon!

Thanks to the team at Zondervan for all the hard work in making this book all it can be. We appreciate you guys and look forward to more projects!

And to all our friends and family who have lent listening ears, helped watch Ember, given constructive feedback, or simply encouraged us to tell our story—thank you!

NOTES

Prologue

1. Brooks & Dunn, "Red Dirt Road," lyrics by Kix Brooks and Ronnie Dunn, April 2003.

Chapter 1: A Patient Pursuit

1. See "Ape Caves," Washington Trails Association, www.wta .org/go-hiking/hikes/ape-cave.
2. Nicholas Sparks, *The Last Song* (New York: Hachette, 2009), 206.
3. Bruce Lee, "#24 Poetry: Love Is Like a Friendship Caught on Fire," December 14, 2016, www.brucelee.com/podcast -blog/2016/12/14/24-poetry.

Chapter 3: Every Wall Must Fall

1. Henry Cloud and John Townsend, *Boundaries with Kids* (Grand Rapids: Zondervan, 1998), 72.

Chapter 4: A Creative Type of Love

1. Gary Chapman, *The Five Love Languages: The Secret to Love That Lasts* (1992: repr., Chicago: Northwood, 2015). To take

the free test and discover your own love languages, visit www
.5lovelanguages.com.

Chapter 5: The Way Forward

1. "The Challenger: Enneagram Type Eight," The Enneagram
   Institute, www.enneagraminstitute.com/type-8, italics original.
2. "The Peacemaker: Enneagram Type Nine," The Enneagram
   Institute, www.enneagraminstitute.com/type-9, italics original.
3. "Enneagram Type Eight (the Challenger) *with* Enneagram
   Type Nine (the Peacemaker)," The Enneagram Institute, www
   .enneagraminstitute.com/relationship-type-8-with-type-9.
4. Timothy Keller, *The Meaning of Marriage: Facing the
   Complexities of Commitment with the Wisdom of God* (New
   York: Riverhead, 2011), 101.

Chapter 6: The Principle of Sharing

1. Sheldon Vanauken, *A Severe Mercy* (San Francisco:
   HarperSanFrancisco, 1987), 35.
2. Vanauken, *A Severe Mercy*, 35.
3. Vanauken, *A Severe Mercy*, 37.
4. Keller, *Meaning of Marriage*, 109.

Chapter 7: Losing the Purity Battle

1. Mary Pickford, *Why Not Try God?* (1934; repr., Culver City,
   CA: Northern Road, 2013), 26.
2. See C. S. Lewis, *Mere Christianity* (1943; repr., New York:
   Macmillan, 1960), 54.
3. Charles Duhigg, *The Power of Habit: Why We Do What We
   Do in Life and Business* (New York: Random House, 2012), 19.
4. We go into more detail about this journal approach in

chapter 11. Our journal is called *The Marriage Journal: Connect, Communicate, and Grow in Love*, and you can read more about it at www.TheMarriageJournal.com.

Part 3: The Big Question

1. See chapter 11 for more detail about this marriage journal session.

Chapter 8: Preparing for the Promise

1. This phrase comes from Sheldon Vanauken, who described his journey of grief following his wife's death as "the Illumination of the Past"—in which he decided to take a careful look at all the books, journals, photos, and poems of their life together as a way to keep their memories alive (see *A Severe Mercy*, 187, 191–92).

2. John Mark Comer, *Loveology: God, Love, Marriage, Sex, and the Never-Ending Story of Male and Female* (Grand Rapids: Zondervan, 2013), 72, italics original.

Chapter 9: Our Code of Conflict

1. Terri Clark, "I Just Wanna Be Mad," lyrics by Kelley Lovelace and Lee Thomas Miller, August 2002.

2. Gary Chapman, "Discover Your Love Language: Quality Time," *Five Love Languages*, www.5lovelanguages.com/languages/quality-time.

3. Vanauken, *A Severe Mercy*, 43.

4. See "20 Important Emotional Affair Statistics," Health Research Funding, https://healthresearchfunding.org/20-important-emotional-affair-statistics.

5. Nicholas Sparks, *The Notebook* (New York: Warner, 1996), 160.

Chapter 10: The Road to Oneness

1. Annie Dillard, *The Writing Life* (1989; repr., New York: HarperCollins, 2013), 32.

Chapter 11: Protect Your Love

1. See Henry Cloud and John Townsend, *Boundaries in Marriage* (Grand Rapids: Zondervan, 1999), 17.
2. Cloud and Townsend, *Boundaries in Marriage*, 17.
3. Charles Spurgeon, *The Power of Prayer in a Believer's Life* (Lynnwood, WA: Emerald, 1993), 15.
4. Timothy Keller, *Prayer: Experiencing Awe and Intimacy with God* (New York: Penguin, 2014), 18.